Autism as a Superpower : What Your Autistic Child Wants You to Know but Can't Say

© 2026 by PNDULUM LLC. All rights reserved.

No part of this book may be reproduced, stored in a retrieval system, or transmitted in any form or by any means, electronic, mechanical, photocopying, recording, or otherwise, without the prior written permission of the publisher, except in the case of brief quotations embodied in critical articles and reviews.

Published by PNDULUM LLC
11700 W. Charleston Blvd. #170
Las Vegas, NV 89135

ISBN: 979-8-218-90351-0

First Edition: September 2025

Publisher's Note: This book is a work of nonfiction. While every effort has been made to ensure its accuracy, the information contained within is provided on an "as is" basis. The author and publisher disclaim any liability in connection with the use of this information.

Printed in the United States of America

For permission requests, speaking inquiries, information about special discounts for bulk purchases please contact:

PNDULUM LLC at hello@pndulum.com

Disclaimer: The information contained in this book is for general informational purposes only. The author and publisher make no representations or warranties of any kind with respect to the accuracy, applicability, or completeness of the contents of this book. The information provided does not constitute professional advice and should not be relied upon as such.

Readers are advised to consult with a qualified professional before making any decisions based on the content of this book. The author and publisher shall not be held liable for any loss or damages arising from the use of the information contained herein.
No guarantee of performance is made or implied. The results achieved through the strategies and advice provided in this book may vary depending on individual circumstances and efforts.

Table of Contents

Introduction

Part I: Please Don't Mistake My Differences for Defiance

- **Chapter 1: I'm Not Broken. I'm Just Wired Differently**
  What you call "misbehavior" is often my nervous system asking for help.

- **Chapter 2: My Superpowers Are Real—So Are My Storms**
  I can shine and struggle in the same hour—both can be true.

Part II: When I Melt Down, I'm Not Trying to Win. I'm Trying to Survive.

- **Chapter 3: My Meltdowns Aren't Tantrums**
  When I lose control, I need safety, fewer demands, and a path back to calm.

- **Chapter 4: When I Get Aggressive, It's a Red Alert—Not My Character**
  If I'm hitting or breaking things, something is dangerously overwhelming—here's how to protect everyone.

- **Chapter 5: My Body Can't Filter the World**
  Sounds, lights, textures, and transitions can hurt—so I fight, flee, or freeze.

- **Chapter 6: If I Run, I'm Not Being Bad—I'm Escaping**
  Elopement is my emergency exit—build layers of prevention, not punishment.

Part III: My Autism Lives Inside a Whole Family

- **Chapter 7: My Siblings Love Me… and They Get Hurt Too**
  Protect my childhood while protecting me—without making anyone the villain.

- **Chapter 8: I Can Feel Your Marriage Straining**
  Stress turns partners into coworkers—here's how to stay united when life is on fire.

- **Chapter 9: I Changed Your Career—and I Know You Miss Yourself.**
  I didn't mean to take your future hostage. But I know my needs rewrote your days—and I see what it cost you.

- **Chapter 10: People Think I'm Naughty. You Feel Judged. I Feel Unsafe**
  Public shame fuels private burnout—use scripts, exits, and boundaries that protect dignity.

- **Chapter 11: Friends Disappear. I Notice.**
  Isolation isn't your imagination—rebuild community with people who can handle our reality.

- **Chapter 12: "School Meetings Make You Fight. I Just Want to Belong**
  Turn IEP battles into a plan that actually works for my brain—and our family's peace.

Part IV: The Future Is Heavy in Your Chest

- **Chapter 13: I Hear You Worry About When You're Gone**
  Make a future file that protects me—and gives you oxygen now

- **Chapter 14: Independence Isn't One Thing**
  My "independence" may be supported, shared, or staged—and it can still be a good life

Part V: When Love Isn't Enough, Systems Must Change

- **Chapter 15: My Needs Evolve as I Develop; Our Family Support System Should Too**
  Growth changes the child—and it must change the system around me

- **Chapter 16: If I Need Residential Care, I Still Need to Be Yours**
  Sometimes structure saves us—how to choose care without losing our connection

- **Chapter 17: Find Out What I'm Built For.**
  Follow my interests to unlock my "superpowers" - learning, confidence, and real sense of belonging

- **Chapter 18: Build Our Family Operating System**
  Turn chaos into a repeatable plan—so our home runs on clarity, not crisis

Closing: Thank You for Learning My Language.

Appendices

- **A. Urban Parenting - The City Protocols**

- **B. Is My Child on the Spectrum? (a parent observation checklist)**

- **C. De-escalation scripts (what to say / what not to say)**

- **D. Sensory audit checklist (home + outings)**

- **E. School/IEP meeting prep sheet**

Introduction

Learning to See What Others Miss

If you're reading this, autism has likely entered your family in a way that no brochure, diagnosis, or checklist could ever fully explain. You may recognize the bright moments first—your child's memory, honesty, intensity, unique humor, or unusual brilliance. What most people don't see are the hidden costs: the nights that stretch too long, the mornings that begin already tense, the public moments that feel like scrutiny, the school meetings that leave you depleted, and the quiet, ever-present question that follows you everywhere—*what happens next?*

This book was written because for too long, the autism conversation has been incomplete.

Over the past three years, I have immersed myself in research that goes beyond surface explanations. Not just clinical literature, but the lived realities of autistic children and the families who love them. I have listened to parents in moments of exhaustion and honesty. I have studied patterns that repeat across households, cities, schools, and stages of development. And I have paid close attention to something that is rarely centered: how autism is *experienced* from the inside, especially by children who do not yet have the language to explain what is happening to them. Again and again, I encountered the same problem—not a lack of love, not a lack of effort, but a lack of translation.

This book is written the way it is—often through the voice of the child—for one reason: to **translate**. Many autistic children cannot always explain, in clean adult language, what is happening inside their bodies and minds. But that does not mean they are silent. The body speaks. Behavior speaks. Withdrawal speaks. Intensity speaks. What parents are often missing is not commitment, but a working language that helps them understand what those signals actually mean.

The chapters ahead are designed to give you that language. Not only what to do, but why it works. Not only how to respond, but what your child is communicating in the first place.

You will see hard truths named plainly: how meltdowns ripple through an entire household, how siblings can be quietly wounded, how marriage strain turns partners into logistical coworkers, how school systems can push parents into constant advocacy battles, and how worry about the future can slowly steal peace from the present. These realities are not exaggerated. They are common. And they are rarely spoken about honestly.

But this book does not stop at recognition. It offers structure where there is chaos, clarity where there is confusion, and tools where there has too often been shame. You will find practical strategies, de-escalation language that protects dignity, and family systems that help your home function on predictability rather than crisis. *This is not a book that asks you to simply "accept" autism and then figure everything out on your own. It is a book that respects the full weight of your reality—and still insists that there is a better way to support it.* **The goal is not to erase autism. The goal is to build a life that fits your child's nervous system, strengthens your family system, and allows your child to grow into the fullest version of who they already are.**

If you are exhausted, you are not failing. You are carrying something heavy without enough structure around it. If you've quietly feared that this diagnosis automatically means your child will have a smaller life, I want you to hold one idea gently as we begin: *a different brain can still become a powerful brain*—especially when someone finally learns how it works.

My own path into this work did not begin in a clinic or a textbook alone. It emerged through years of building systems designed to improve the human experience, and later through close collaboration with autism care professionals who have worked with thousands of children and families. Together, this dual perspective—clinical depth paired with systems thinking—has revealed something essential: autism does not require less ambition, less hope, or less expectation. It requires *better alignment* between the child, the family, and the environment surrounding them. That belief underpins everything in this book.

You may be a parent still reeling from a recent diagnosis, trying to make sense of acronyms and treatment options that feel overwhelming. You may be years into the journey, carrying invisible scars from daily meltdowns, sleepless nights, and endless negotiations with schools or insurance companies. Or you may be somewhere in between—longing for hope while navigating the very real demands this path places on your family.

Wherever you are, I want to say this clearly: **you are not alone.**

I have listened to hundreds of parents who love their autistic children fiercely and still admit, often in whispers, that they are exhausted. Parents who have sacrificed careers, friendships, and health to keep their families afloat. Parents who feel guilt for wishing things were easier, and shame because the world judges them for even having that thought. The outside world rarely sees the full picture. They may see your child's brilliance in public, but not the private toll on your household. They may admire your strength, without understanding how close you sometimes feel to the edge. And they almost never see how deeply you worry about the future—about independence, safety, belonging, and who will care for your child when you no longer can.

Autism is not a handicap. It is a different wiring of the human brain. Yes, it can bring struggle—sometimes intense struggle. But within those same differences are strengths, sensitivities, and capabilities that can become extraordinary when they are supported intelligently. The real challenge is not autism itself. The challenge is surviving its storms while building a family life in which *everyone*—your child, siblings, your marriage, and you—can thrive.

If you have ever felt like your family was close to breaking under the weight of autism, you are not broken. You are human. And you are exactly the kind of parent your child needs. This book is here to dismantle one of the most harmful myths of all: the idea that autism automatically equals limitation. It is here to offer a new lens, a clearer map, and a path forward that honors both struggle and potential.

This book is for you.

Part I: Please Don't Mistake My Differences for Defiance.

Chapter 1: I'm Not Broken. I'm Just Wired Differently.

The word *handicap* has been a shadow over autism for decades. It's whispered in school meetings, implied in medical reports, and stamped on government forms. It suggests deficiency, limitation, and a life defined by what cannot be done.

But here's the truth: **autism is not a handicap.** It is a difference.

This doesn't mean it's easy. Parents on the frontlines know the reality: children who bolt into traffic, who lash out at siblings, who push marriages to the brink. Families who lose friends because outings are too unpredictable, or who live in homes where every door and drawer must be locked for safety. These are not "quirks." They are daily battles that take extraordinary resilience to endure.

Yet to call autism a handicap is to miss the other half of the story. Because the very wiring that creates meltdowns in a supermarket can also create extraordinary focus in art, music, or coding. The same brain that resists small talk may thrive on radical honesty. The child who struggles in traditional classrooms may grow into an adult who reimagines industries, invents new technologies, or sees patterns no one else notices.

History is full of autistic voices—though they often went unnamed. From scientists like Nikola Tesla to artists like Michelangelo, from activists to innovators like Elon Musk who publicly revealed on Saturday Night Live that he has a form of Asperger's syndrome sparking conversations about neurodiversity in leadership and the perceived strengths (like deep focus) and challenges (like social cues) associated with autism. Autism has shaped the world more than most realize. Even today, countless autistic adults speak openly of the strengths hidden in their differences.

But before we can celebrate those superpowers, we have to tell the truth about the storms. Because for families right now, autism often feels less like a gift and more like a breaking point.

One father on a parenting forum described it this way:

> *"I've thrown my lucrative career into the dirt to help my son. We have excellent therapists. We've read all the books. Yet he's becoming more aggressive, more unlikeable by the month. My wife and I love him, but we are exhausted. I see the fractures growing in our marriage, and I fear we won't make it."*

This isn't failure. This is the cost of living in a world that doesn't yet know how to support neurodiverse families. The endless appointments, the lack of respite, the judgment from strangers—these wear parents down until they start to believe the myth themselves: *maybe my child is too broken; maybe we as a family are too weak.*

The first step in reclaiming your family's future is to shatter that lie. Autism does not equal brokenness. It equals difference. And difference, though hard, is not a death sentence.

In the chapters ahead, we'll explore how to protect your family from crisis, how to preserve your marriage, how to honor siblings, and how to find your tribe. We'll also look at the tools to uncover your child's strengths so that the storms don't erase the brilliance hidden within.

But before we go further, I want you to carry this anchor: **Your child is not a handicap. Your family is not a failure. And you are not alone in this fight.** Because autism—though it will test you—can also be a superpower.

The Acute Reality Parents Rarely Say Out Loud

Some families are dealing with occasional dysregulation. Other families are living with acute, relentless intensity—daily or hourly storms that change everything.

Parents describe it like hypervigilance: living in a constant state of dread, waiting for the next explosion—especially when elopement, aggression, or dangerous behaviors exist. Some of you have lived through situations the outside world can't imagine—like violent episodes, feces smearing, doors breaking, bolting toward traffic, or events so intense they change your nervous system too.

And then society tells you things like:

- "Just discipline them."
- "They need structure."
- "If you'd stop giving in…"
- "Kids don't run the house."

But here's what you already know; you are not dealing with a typical defiance problem. You are dealing with a nervous system problem. This book will give you the strategies needed to not just cope with autism, but harness the advantages it offers to exceed expectations for your child's development.

To truly understand and prepare your child for the best possible life, you need to hear directly from them. To take a moment to step fully inside the experience within their minds and immerse yourself into their world. Moving forward, this book adopts the child's perspective—giving voice to their struggles, concerns, and most critical needs. This intentional dialogue is designed to equip you, the caregiver or parent, with the necessary empathy to bring out their greatest potential.

・・・

Three Moments You've Probably Lived (And What I Wish You Knew)

1) Hair Washing: "It's Just Hair" (But it's not)

You turn on the water. I tense before you even touch me. You try to be gentle. I still panic. You think: "Why is this such a big deal?"

But what you can't feel is what I feel:
- water pressure is painful
- the sound is amplified
- water in my face triggers fear
- the sensation is unpredictable
- I can't tell when it will stop
- I can't control the sequence

Parents describe hair washing and medical routines as so traumatic that it can cause **weeks of behavioral regression** afterward. If I could speak clearly in that moment, I might say:

"Please don't force my body through panic. Teach my body safety slowly. Give me control." What helps isn't "tough love." What helps is **predictability, consent, and gradual exposure**.

Not because you're spoiling me— because you're teaching my nervous system that care is not an attack.

2) The Doctor: "Stop fighting me" (But I'm not fighting you)

The waiting room smells like chemicals. The lights hum. The chairs are scratchy. People talk too loud. My body is bracing like something bad is going to happen. Then someone reaches for me. Someone touches me. Someone restrains me. And my body does what bodies do when they feel trapped. It fights.

Parents describe doctor visits as traumatic because the child experiences it as overwhelming and violating—especially when the child cannot reliably communicate or predict what's happening. If I could translate myself, I might say:

"I need you to prepare me. Show me what will happen. Let me practice. Give me a safe escape plan."

You don't have to make me love the doctor. You just have to make it survivable— and then repeat survivable until it becomes tolerable.

3) Public Meltdowns: "They think you're a bad parent" (And I feel that)

In public, the pressure doubles. Because now it's not only my discomfort— it's your embarrassment. Your fear of judgment. Your sense of being watched. And I can feel it. Even if I can't name it. When people think I'm "naughty," you feel judged, and I feel unsafe. Sometimes parents describe this as paranoia—feeling the judgment in public when their child is "being autistic" and others interpret it as bad behavior. Here's what I wish you could know. **Your shame doesn't calm me. It spikes me.** Because when you become tight, sharp, urgent, embarrassed— my nervous system reads that as danger. If I could speak clearly, I'd say:

"Protect me from their eyes. Don't perform for strangers. Help me exit. Help me recover."

The Translation Every Parent Deserves

Here is the truth that changes everything:

A meltdown is not a tantrum. It doesn't end because you "win." It ends when my nervous system returns to baseline. So when you see behavior, try this translation:

Behavior → Need (Quick Translation Guide)

- **I'm screaming** → my body is overloaded; I can't process language right now
- **I'm hitting/throwing** → something feels unbearable; I need safety + fewer demands
- **I'm running** → I'm escaping sensory overwhelm or fear (not "being bad")
- **I'm refusing** → the request is too big, too fast, too unclear, or too painful
- **I'm shutting down** → I'm flooded; I need low stimulation + time + gentleness
- **I'm "fine at school" but explode at home** → masking all day; home is where I finally release

This doesn't remove consequences. It changes *how* you approach the moment - you become a **guide** instead of a combatant.

What I Need Most (If I Could Tell You Clearly)

1) I need less talking—more clarity

When I'm escalating, language becomes noise. In the moment, I need:
- fewer words
- simple choices
- calm tone
- predictable sequence

If you want to help me, speak like you're guiding someone through smoke. Not lectures. No explanations. Just: **safe steps.**

2) I need you to believe my nervous system is real

I'm not "making it up." My sensory world can be painful. My transitions can feel like threats. My uncertainty can feel like free-fall. When you treat this like an attitude, I feel misunderstood. When you treat this like biology, I feel protected.

3) I need a plan, not a reaction

When life is improvised, I become unpredictable. When life is patterned, I become learnable.

I need:
- visual routines
- transition warnings
- predictable "first/then" structures
- rehearsed exit plans
- a calm-down space that isn't punishment

This is how you teach me regulation. Not through pressure—through structure.

4) I need you to protect my dignity in public

Please don't narrate me in front of strangers. Please don't argue about me while I'm melting down. Please don't let the world turn me into a spectacle. I need you to be my shield—quietly.

5) I need you to keep loving me without becoming my prisoner

This is the part you don't say out loud, but I feel it. You're terrified you will disappear inside my needs. You're afraid your marriage will break. You worry about siblings growing up in the shadow of my storms. You miss your old self. You feel guilty for missing your old life. I need you to know something important - **I don't need you to burn down your life to prove you love me.** I need you to build something sustainable, because sustainability is what keeps you here, long enough for me to grow.

The Message Behind the Pain

Here is the part that might surprise you. Even when I can't communicate well... I can still feel love. I can still feel fear. I can still feel your nervous system.

I notice:
- when you flinch
- when you brace
- when you're exhausted
- when you're angry at the world
- when you're blaming yourself
- when you're trying your best

And if I had words big enough to carry the truth, I would tell you this:

I don't need you to be perfect. I need you to be steady.
I don't need you to win. I need you to help me feel safe.
I don't need you to erase autism. I need you to translate it.

Because my brain is not broken. It's different. And different brains need different care. That's not a tragedy. That's a design challenge—one our family can learn to solve.

Chapter 2: My Superpowers Are Real—So Are My Storms

You live in two realities at once.

In one reality, you're tired in a way that doesn't have a clean ending. It's not just "busy parents tired." It's the kind of tiredness that sinks into your bones because the day starts like a sprint and ends like a rescue mission. You might be up before the sun, already negotiating the first battle—clothes, teeth, breakfast, shoes—while the rest of the world imagines mornings are simply a routine. By the time you reach the car, or the sidewalk, or the train platform, you're already drained. And you haven't even lived the day yet.

In the other reality, you're holding something rare in your hands. You're watching a mind that notices what other minds skip. You're seeing memory, pattern, honesty, intensity, creativity—sometimes so sharp it takes your breath away. You can be shaken by the chaos and stunned by the brilliance in the same hour. Both realities are true. If you deny the struggle, you betray your own lived experience. If you ignore the strengths, you miss who I actually am.

This chapter is about learning to hold both truths without letting either one swallow the other. Because here's what I need you to understand: my storms are real, but they aren't my identity. And my gifts are real, but they aren't a magic spell that cancels out the hard parts. **Autism can magnify both ends of the spectrum—the struggle and the strength.**

The part you don't get to see from the outside

When I melt down, it can look like defiance from ten feet away. It can look like I'm choosing to be difficult. It can look like I'm trying to "win." But most of the time, what's actually happening is that my body has crossed a line you can't see.

I might be fighting a tag in my shirt that feels like sandpaper. I might be hearing the refrigerator hum like a siren. I might be trying to translate your words while my brain is also tracking the brightness of the lights, the smell of the hallway, the unpredictability of what comes next, and the fact that I don't know how to explain any of that fast enough. And when I can't explain it, my nervous system speaks for me.

That's the storm.

It's not pretty. It's not convenient. And it can be terrifying—especially when it comes with aggression, screaming, bolting, or destruction. You're not imagining how intense it is. You're not weak for feeling like you want to collapse on the kitchen floor and cry. That reaction is human. But I need you to know something else at the same time: the storm is not the whole weather system. It's not the whole climate of who I am.

Why my strengths disappear when you're in survival mode

When the living room looks like a tornado passed through it, nobody feels like celebrating anything. When you're getting calls from school, when you're facing yet another suspension, when you're bracing for the next public incident—your mind narrows. It has to. Stress forces you to focus on the emergency right in front of you. And the world helps that narrowing along.

Schools, doctors, even extended family can accidentally train you to view me through a deficit lens—what I can't do, won't do, fail to do. The result is subtle but devastating: you start describing me as a crisis instead of a person with capacity. That's how families lose hope. Not because hope is irrational—but because hope gets buried under paperwork, incidents, and exhaustion. So here's the pivot: we don't pretend the storms are small. We get honest about them. But we also stop letting the storms become the only story you tell yourself about me.

A real-life example: the "battle morning" and the hidden signal underneath

Let me show you how this can work without turning into fake positivity.

Picture a morning you've lived before. You're trying to get out the door. I'm stuck on something that makes no sense to anyone else—my sock seam is wrong, my shirt feels "angry," the schedule changed, the sound of the hair dryer is too much, the toothpaste burns, the backpack zipper is loud. You're counting minutes. I'm counting sensations. You say, "We're late." My body hears, "You're trapped." And then the storm comes. From the outside, the story is: *He can't even get dressed without screaming.* But now let's slow it down and look closer.

The hidden signal might be this: **I notice fairness, exactness, and mismatch like it's a fire alarm.** I can tell when something is uneven, inconsistent, or "off." *That same sensitivity that makes me melt down over one wrong detail is also the sensitivity that makes me brilliant at systems, patterns, maps, music, language, coding, mechanics—anything with structure.* In some kids it shows up as memorizing movie scripts or building intricate worlds; in others it's recalling every bus route in a city like it's a personal library.

So your job isn't to say, "This isn't hard." Your job is to say, "This is hard—and it's telling us something." That's not denial; that's intelligence.

Reframing without lying to yourself

Reframing is not a motivational poster. It's a tool. It doesn't erase the meltdown; it changes the meaning you attach to it so you can respond with strategy instead of despair.

Here is how it sounds in real life:

» You name the struggle honestly:
>Dinner is impossible. I can't get him to sit without screaming.

»Then you search for the strength hiding nearby:

>He has a fierce sense of fairness and order; he notices every imbalance, every unexpected change, every rule violation—down to one extra French fry.

» Then you ask how to cultivate that strength, not just survive it:

>What if he helps set the dinner rules? What if the "fairness radar" becomes a job he's proud of, instead of a force we fight every night?

You're not excusing harmful behavior but rather decoding the nervous system and retrieving the gift that's tangled up in it.

A second real-life example: the marriage on the edge and the drum kit that saved a doorway

A father once described something that a lot of people won't say out loud: his son's aggression nearly ended his marriage. Not because they didn't love their child, but because the household felt like it was always one incident away from breaking. The storms didn't leave space for recovery. They lived on alert. Then they noticed something.

That same intensity—too big, too loud, too explosive when it hit a demand—showed up differently when the boy sat at a drum kit. The father said that when his son played, it was like his soul finally had a clean doorway out of his body. The force that terrified them in the living room became rhythm, repetition, release. The nervous system that looked like chaos became music.

That doesn't mean drumming "fixed" autism. It means the family found an outlet where the intensity could be expressed safely, skillfully, even beautifully—rather than only through crisis. *That's what I mean when I say my superpowers are real.* They're often sitting right next to the storm, wearing the same face.

What I want you to do with this, starting now

I want you to become a collector of evidence—not just evidence of what's hard, but evidence of what's true. Because you will have days where the struggle screams louder than the strength. Those are the days you'll be tempted to believe the deficit story: *This is all there is. This is who my child will always be. This is the end of my life as I knew it.*

On those days, you need receipts that argue back. You can build that evidence in simple ways: by writing down one strength you notice each day so your brain doesn't erase the wins; by protecting space for passions so therapy doesn't become the entire identity of our family; by making sure school plans don't only list deficits but also describe what lights me up and how I learn best; by helping siblings understand that the hard parts are real, but so is the shine—so resentment doesn't become the silent inheritance in your home.

None of this is sentimental. It's structural. It's how you build a family narrative that can carry weight.

Closing reflection

Every parent of an autistic child lives in tension between crisis and capability. That tension is not a sign you're failing. It's the landscape you're learning to navigate. *You are not failing me.*

When you start seeing the superpowers behind the struggles, you don't just give me hope—you give yourself stamina. You stop parenting like you're trying to extinguish a fire that never ends, and you start parenting like you're guiding a nervous system toward safety while building a life that fits who I actually am. I'm not asking you to pretend it's easy. I'm asking you to remember the whole truth:

Behind every meltdown is a nervous system in overdrive. And behind every intense interest, every unusual focus, every "why is my kid like this?" moment—there may be the seed of a gift that can mature into something strong, stable, and real.

My storms are real. But so are my superpowers. Hold both. And **keep going**.

Part II: When I Melt Down, I'm Not Trying to Win. I'm Trying to Survive.

Chapter 3: My Meltdowns Aren't Tantrums

When the World Falls Apart in Your Living Room

If you are parenting an autistic child, you know that meltdowns are not the same thing as tantrums. Tantrums end when the child gets what they want. **Meltdowns end when the nervous system calms down.** That's a huge difference—and one that the outside world rarely understands.

For many families, meltdowns are not occasional flare-ups; they're daily, sometimes hourly realities. The sound of clattering furniture, screams echoing down hallways, or the panic that comes when a child bolts toward the street—all of this can make parents live in a constant state of hypervigilance.

In one of our parent onboardings, a mother described how her teenage son would "smear feces on the walls, break the doors, and then run into traffic." Another parent shared about their younger child, who "launched into such intense meltdowns that even hair washing became traumatic for weeks afterward." These are not rare outliers. They are common, lived realities.

This chapter is about naming those realities, validating the exhaustion you feel, and giving you practical playbooks to turn chaos into safety and—over time—growth.

Understanding What's Really Happening

A meltdown is not a choice. It's the body and brain's survival response to overwhelm. Here's a simple breakdown:

1. **Trigger (Antecedent):** A demand, a sensory overload, or an unexpected change.

2. **Explosion (Behavior):** Screaming, hitting, running, breaking, biting, self-harm.

3. **Aftermath (Consequence):** Exhaustion, shame, regression, or withdrawal.

The key is this: **your child is not giving you a hard time—they're having a hard time.** That perspective shift doesn't make the screaming easier in the moment, but it gives you the clarity to respond as a guide, not a combatant.

Safety First: Making Home Crisis-Proof

Your first responsibility is not to "fix" the meltdown—it's to keep everyone safe.

Steps to Crisis-Proof Your Home:

- **Anchor furniture.** Bookshelves, TVs, and heavy dressers should be mounted to walls. Meltdowns often involve pushing or climbing.

- **Remove weapons of opportunity.** Lock up scissors, kitchen knives, tools, lighters, and anything that can be thrown or used dangerously.

- **Create a safe zone.** Designate a room or corner with soft surfaces (beanbags, crash pads, blankets). Teach your child this is their "cool-down space."

- **Install simple safety gates and locks.** Prevent elopement (running away) by using childproof locks at doors and windows—even for older children.

- **Have an exit plan.** If aggression escalates beyond safe limits, siblings should know exactly where to go (neighbor's house, safe room).

You wouldn't judge a parent for childproofing outlets when a toddler is crawling. Meltdown-proofing for an autistic child is the same principle: it's love translated into safety.

De-Escalation Playbook (Step by Step)

When the meltdown is already happening, here's a sequence you can follow:

1. Lower the Demands Immediately
Stop talking. Stop correcting. Stop teaching. Demands only add fuel.

2. Control Your Own Body
Soften your posture. Keep your voice calm. Avoid eye contact if it escalates agitation.

3. Minimize the Audience
Remove siblings or other children from the scene. The fewer people present, the faster the storm can pass.

4. Create Space, Not Confrontation
Stand at a safe distance but block exits if elopement is a risk. Give options for safe movement.

5. Offer Regulating Tools (Only if Accepted)
Weighted blanket, favorite fidget, headphones, cold drink—offer calmly, but don't force.

6. Ride the Wave

Remind yourself: this will end. Meltdowns can last 10 minutes or 2 hours, but they do end.

7. Recovery Ritual

When calm returns, don't rehash. Offer comfort: "That was hard. You're safe now." Later, when everyone is calm, you can teach and process.

Not every meltdown is dangerous, but many are. Parents share stories of being bitten, punched, or choked by their children. These are devastating experiences—especially when society tells you to "just discipline better."

What to Do in Violent Episodes:

- **Stay physically safe.** Use arm shields, block with pillows, or step back.

- **Call for help if necessary.** If violence escalates beyond safe control, you are not a failure for dialing 911 or crisis lines.

- **Have a "Safe Word" with Siblings.** Teach siblings to exit quickly when the word is said.

- **Document for Support.** Keep logs of severe episodes—these can help in getting services, insurance coverage, or emergency respite.

Important: Aggression is not your child's character. It is their nervous system at war with itself. Your role is to keep everyone safe while working with professionals to reduce triggers and build coping skills.

The Hidden Cost: Parent PTSD

Many parents confessed to trauma. "I flinch every time he raises his hand—even when he's just reaching for the fridge," one wrote. Others described living in a state of dread, waiting for the next explosion. This is real. Parents of autistic children with severe behaviors often develop PTSD symptoms: hypervigilance, intrusive memories, and even depression.

What Helps:

- **Respite care.** Even two hours of relief can restore equilibrium.

- **Parent peer groups.** Being around people who *get it* breaks isolation.

- **Therapy for parents.** Your trauma matters too. Taking care of your mental health is not selfish—it's survival.

Teaching Recovery & Resilience

Meltdowns don't just affect the parent—they affect siblings. One adult sibling shared with us: "I was writing suicide notes at seven because my autistic brother's violence was destroying our home." That's a gut punch that no parent ever expects to hear. So, in order protect siblings and rebuild resilience amongst the family implement these practices during meltdown-related events:

- **Validate openly.** Don't minimize the episode. Say plainly and honestly, "I know it's scary when your brother/sister gets upset."

- **Protect proactively.** Give siblings safe exit strategies.

- **Carve sibling-only time.** This is critical; the quality-of-time matters far more than the amount; even 20 minutes a day signals: "You matter too."

- **Teach them perspective.** Help them see their autistic sibling's strengths, not just their challenges.

Beyond the Family: Working With Schools, Police & Systems

One mother shared with us that her son's high school refused to re-enroll him after he pushed a pregnant teacher. Another parent described calling 911 during a violent episode and watching officers arrive untrained, escalating rather than helping. This is the reality: these systems often fail autistic children during crises for lack of knowledge and skills related to autistic episodes.

Practical Steps You Can Take Today to Prepare:

- **Crisis Plans with Schools.** Work with IEP teams to develop meltdown protocols. Insist on demonstrable staff training specific to ABA-related incidents.

- **Local Crisis Teams.** Some cities and counties have mobile crisis intervention teams—program their numbers into your phone.

- **First Responder Cards.** Create a laminated card explaining your child's diagnosis and calming strategies to hand to police or EMTs.

Remember that your voice as a parent matters. Systems change when parents push for it, relentlessly as a united voice.

Long-Term Crisis Prevention

While some meltdowns are unavoidable, many can be reduced with proactive strategies. Here are proactive strategies to help with prevention:

- **Sensory Diet:** Regular sensory input (swings, trampolines, weighted vests).

- **Predictable Routines:** Implement visual schedules around the house, and protocols surrounding transition warnings.

- **Communication Supports:** AAC devices, picture cards, or simple sign language to reduce in-the-moment frustration.

- **Behavior Tracking:** Note patterns (time of day, environment, triggers). Share with therapists.

The goal is not perfection—it's to lower the baseline stress so meltdowns are fewer, shorter, and safer.

The Hope in the Storm

It's easy to feel that meltdowns will define your child's life forever. But countless families report that with time, structure, and the right supports, meltdowns do decrease. One father recently commented : "At 10 years old, my son's meltdowns were daily and violent. At 17, they still happen, but now he can recognize them coming and ask for his headphones." That progression is the hope: not that the storms disappear overnight, but that your child learns to steer their own ship a little more each year.

Action Steps for Parents (Quick Reference)

- **Crisis-Proof Your Home**: anchor furniture, lock hazards, set safe zones.

- **Use the De-Escalation Playbook**: stop demands, stay calm, create space, ride the wave.

- **Protect Siblings**: safe words, safe exits, carve out one-on-one time.

- **Document Episodes**: for insurance, schools, and services.

- **Seek Respite & Support**: you can't pour from an empty cup.

- **Plan with Schools & First Responders**: insist on crisis plans and staff training.

- **Track & Prevent**: log triggers, build sensory diets, support communication.

Closing Reflection

Meltdowns and crisis episodes may be the hardest part of raising an autistic child. They leave you shaken, exhausted, sometimes even afraid. But they do not mean your child is hopeless, or that your family is doomed.

Autism is a superpower because behind the storm is a brain wired differently—often capable of astonishing creativity, honesty, and passion. Your role as a parent is not to extinguish the storms but to build the harbor strong enough to withstand them, and to teach your child to sail.

With time, tools, and a supportive community, the storms become fewer, the waters calmer, and the superpowers clearer.

Chapter 4: When I Get Aggressive, It's a Red Alert—Not My Character

How to stay safe, de-escalate fast, and build a calmer home without surrendering your authority

There's a kind of fear that doesn't announce itself with sirens. It creeps in later—after the door slams, after the neighbor's glance, after you've checked everyone's bodies for bruises and you're standing in the kitchen with your hands shaking, wondering how a normal afternoon turned into a scene you never imagined would happen in your home.

If you've lived through an incident of aggression with your autistic child, you know the particular flavor of it. It isn't just a shock. It's grief, guilt, anger, exhaustion, and something heavier: **the dread that you're failing, that your child is becoming "dangerous," that you're losing control of the household, that siblings are no longer safe**, that your marriage is carrying stress it wasn't built for, that someone is going to judge you—and worst of all, that you might someday have to choose between protecting your child and protecting everyone else.

Let me say this plainly, from the inside of the storm: when I get aggressive, it is not a moral statement about who I am. It is not a declaration that I don't love you. It is not proof that I'm a "bad kid." It's a red alert—*my nervous system hitting the panic button because something in me has moved from stress to threat*. And **when I'm in threat mode, I can look like a different person**.

That doesn't mean you ignore it. It doesn't mean you tolerate harm. It doesn't mean you "let it slide because of autism." No. Safety is sacred. **Boundaries matter**. You can love me fiercely and still stop me firmly. What it *does* mean is that you'll get further—faster—when you treat aggression like an emergency signal you can decode, not a personality flaw you must punish out of me.

This chapter will give you simple core concepts you can actually use: what aggression often *means* in autistic kids, what to do *in the moment*, how to reduce repeat incidents, and how to reset the home after the storm so you don't live on eggshells forever.

The first truth: aggression is usually the last link in a chain

Most parents meet aggression at the end of a long invisible process. You see the shove, the hit, the bite, the thrown object, the kicked wall. But long before that moment, my body has been speaking to you in smaller ways.

I'm not hiding it on purpose. Many of us don't recognize our own escalation until we're already far up the ladder. Or we recognize it but don't have the skills to communicate it. Or we're trying to communicate it, but we don't have words for it, so it comes out sideways.

Aggression is often what happens when:

- I don't have a reliable way to say, "I'm overwhelmed."
- I can't escape what's overwhelming me.
- I'm being pushed to perform while my brain is in overload.
- My body is in pain, fatigue, hunger, or sensory distress and I can't explain it.
- I feel trapped, cornered, shamed, or misunderstood.

In other words, aggression isn't usually the *first* behavior. It's the *final* behavior—what shows up when every earlier message fails.

Your job isn't to become a perfect parent who prevents every outburst. Your job is to become a skilled responder who can see the chain early, interrupt it safely, and teach better pathways over time.

The second truth: you can't "teach a lesson" to a brain in panic

When my nervous system is in fight-or-flight, my thinking brain is offline. That's not an excuse; it's a biological fact. And it's why the usual parenting tools—lectures, long explanations, consequences delivered mid-storm—often fail miserably in the moment. You can't reason me out of a threat response. You can only guide me back into safety. If you want one concept to hold onto when you're overwhelmed, hold this:

De-escalation first. Teaching comes later.

When you try to teach while I'm panicking, I can experience it as pressure. Pressure adds heat. Heat turns to explosion. That's how a parent who wants peace ends up in a power struggle with a nervous system that feels cornered.

The third truth: you're allowed to be firm without being loud

Some parents fear that if they don't "show dominance," aggression will take over. Other parents fear that if they become firm, they'll traumatize their child. The answer isn't softness or force. The answer is *calm authority*.

Calm authority says:
"I will not let you hurt anyone."
and also:
"I will help you get back to control."

It's not pleading. It's not debating. It's not screaming. **It's a steady spine.**

A simple "in-the-moment" playbook you can actually remember

When aggression hits, your brain will want something simple. Not a textbook. Not a flowchart with twenty steps. Something you can do while your heart is pounding.

Here is a sequence you can practice until it becomes instinct. Think of it as **S.A.F.E.**

S — Secure safety first.

If anyone is at immediate risk, create space. Move siblings away. Remove objects that can become projectiles. Increase distance. Position yourself at an angle, not face-to-face like a challenge. If you must block, block with soft barriers (pillows, couch cushions), not your hands swinging back. **Your goal is protection**, not punishment.

A — Adjust demands down.

In escalation, demands act like gasoline. Reduce language. Reduce choices. Reduce expectations. If you were insisting on homework, hygiene, shoes, the car seat, the store—**pause the battle**. The lesson is not worth an injury. You can revisit expectations later when brains are back online.

F — Fewer words, lower voice, slower body.

Your nervous system talks to mine. If you get louder and faster, I feel chased. If you get calmer and slower, my threat meter drops. Use short phrases like:

- "You're safe."
- "I'm here."
- "Hands down."
- "Back up."
- "Breathe."

Skip explanations. Skip "Why are you doing this?" I probably don't know.

E — Exit route and regulation.

- Offer a way out that saves dignity. Not as a reward—as a reset.
- "Break. Room."
- "Couch. Squeeze the pillow."
- "Bathroom. Water on hands."
- "Outside for air."

Give me a safe place to land and a safe body action to do—pressure, deep breathing, wall pushes, heavy blanket, chewing, cold water, paced walking. This is not permissiveness. It's skillful crisis management. If you want one sentence to guide your actions:

"I'm not negotiating right now; I'm restoring safety."

The single biggest mistake in aggressive episodes

Most aggressive incidents get worse when the child feels trapped. Trapped can mean physically blocked in a hallway. It can also mean emotionally trapped: being cornered by words, being forced to talk, being forced to apologize mid-meltdown, being forced to make eye contact, being forced to "act normal" while the body is screaming. If you're in a showdown and my body is climbing, ask yourself **"Where is the trap?"** Then remove it.

Sometimes the trap is a demand I can't meet in that state. Sometimes it's an environment (lights, noise, crowd). Sometimes it's the feeling that I'm losing and you're winning, and my nervous system decides the only escape is fight. **Give me a way to lose the demand without losing dignity, and you'll see fewer explosions.**

Two kinds of aggression (and why it matters)

Not all aggression is the same. If you can tell which kind you're seeing, you'll respond more effectively.

» Overload aggression is "I can't handle this."

It often shows up when there's sensory overwhelm, too much change, too many words, fatigue, hunger, pain, or social stress. The child might look frantic, chaotic, not in control. Afterward, they may seem confused, ashamed, or exhausted.

» Control aggression is "This works for me."

It can develop when aggression reliably ends demands, wins access, or gets attention. This doesn't mean the child is manipulative in a villainous way. It means the behavior has been reinforced—often accidentally—because it got results. In real life, these often blend. An overwhelmed child learns that aggression creates space. Then the brain uses it more quickly next time. Your approach stays grounded either way: protect safety, reduce reinforcement of harm, and teach replacements that actually work.

After the incident: the "repair window" is where progress happens

The most important moment isn't the blow-up. It's what you do when the storm passes and my brain returns. This is when you build the future. If you punish harshly when I'm already ashamed, I learn: *I'm bad.* If you ignore it completely, I learn: *This is just how we do life.* If you repair with calm structure, I learn: *I can come back from this, and there's a better way.* A simple repair conversation can be short. It can be gentle and firm at the same time:

- "Something went wrong. You got too big."
- "I will not let you hit me."
- "Next time, we do 'break' or 'help.'"
- "Let's practice it now."

Then you practice the replacement skill when everyone is calm. You're not lecturing. You're installing a new pathway.

Replacement skills: you are not just stopping aggression—you're giving me an exit

Aggression is often an exit strategy. If you remove it without replacing it, I'll panic harder. The key is to build new exits that are safer and more effective. For many kids, the first replacements need to be **simple and physical**, because when stress rises, language drops.

Some examples:

- A "Break" card (or a single word sign) that always works when used.
- A "Help" card for tasks that feel impossible.
- A "All done" signal for sensory overload moments.
- A regulation routine: squeeze pillow, wall push-ups, heavy blanket, cold water, chew tool, paced walk.

* Here's the rule parents miss: **replacement skills must work every time at the beginning** or the child won't trust them. If I use "break" and you say, "No, finish first," my nervous system learns the new exit is fake. Aggression becomes the only exit that works. Later, once the skill is established, you can shape it: "Break for two minutes, then one problem." But first you build trust that communication beats violence.

The environment is not background noise—it's often the trigger

Many aggressive episodes aren't about defiance, they're about input. You can't out-discipline a sensory system. You can only design around it. Common environment triggers that parents underestimate:

- harsh lighting (especially fluorescents)
- loud HVAC hums or appliances
- crowded rooms with unpredictable movement
- strong smells (cleaners, perfumes, certain foods)
- scratchy clothes, tight waistbands, sock seams
- noise layering (TV + conversation + phone + kitchen sounds)

If aggression clusters in certain places—grocery stores, bathrooms, restaurants, morning routines, the homework table—don't moralize it. Investigate it like a detective. **Ask: what sensory load, what demand load, what transition load is present there?** Sometimes one change saves an entire season of life: headphones, dimmer lights, predictable schedule, visual timer, "first/then" card, snack before errands, transition warnings, clear end times, and through structured choices.

A real-life example: the homework war that stopped being a war

A parent once shared that their child became aggressive most evenings, and they swore it was "attitude." It looked like refusal and disrespect—until they tracked it. The pattern was almost embarrassing in its simplicity: aggression happened on homework nights, especially writing assignments, especially when the parent hovered and corrected. What they changed wasn't a punishment plan. It was the pathway.

They moved homework earlier—before fatigue peaked. They shortened sessions into sprints with timed breaks. They stopped hovering and reduced correction language. They introduced a "help" signal that paused the task without shame. They used a visual checklist so the child could see progress instead of feeling trapped in endlessness. The aggression didn't vanish overnight, but it stopped being nightly. Once safety stabilized they could teach writing skills with less trauma for everyone. This is what I mean when I say: treat my aggression as a red alert, then adjust the system that triggers the alert.

A real-life example: the sibling moment that became a family protocol

In another home, aggression spiked when a younger sibling touched the autistic child's things. It seemed "mean." It felt scary. The parents started separating the kids constantly, and resentment grew. Then they changed the household structure instead of blaming the children. They created a "protected zone" shelf and a visual rule: green items can be shared; red items are private. They taught the autistic child a simple phrase: "Stop. My space." They taught the sibling a simple response: "Okay." They practiced it like a game when everyone was calm—over and over—until the routine became automatic. The goal wasn't perfect kindness. The goal was safety through structure. The aggression didn't disappear completely. But the number of incidents dropped sharply because the child no longer felt constantly invaded—and the sibling no longer felt constantly punished for being a kid.

The parent's nervous system is part of the intervention

This part is hard to hear when you're exhausted, but it's powerful. If you are living on high alert, my body will feel it. If you are constantly bracing for impact, I will interpret the world as dangerous. I'm not saying you caused aggression. I'm saying your regulation is a stabilizer.

That means your own reset matters: stepping away when safe, trading off with another adult, having a script you repeat instead of improvising and practicing the de-escalation voice when you're calm so it's available when you're not. You don't need to be perfect; you need to be consistent.

The boundary that must never move

If there's one line that cannot be blurry, it's this:

Harming people is not allowed.

Not "sometimes." Not "when you're stressed." Not "when you didn't sleep." Not "because of autism." **The boundary is stable**. The compassion lives in how you enforce it. Enforcement doesn't have to mean force. It can mean distance, blocking, moving siblings, ending the activity, removing dangerous objects, pausing demands or calling for professional support. **Your child's brain learns safety through repetition**: "My parents will keep everyone safe, including me."

When you should seek higher-level support immediately

You are not being dramatic for getting help. Always remember that aggression is a safety issue, and never about pride.

Seek professional support urgently if:

- aggression is escalating in severity or frequency
- there are serious injuries, choking attempts, weapon use, or threats
- your child is harming themselves
- siblings are living in fear
- school is calling crisis meetings repeatedly
- you feel afraid you might lose control and respond in a way you regret

Sometimes the missing piece is medical: pain, GI distress, sleep disorders, seizures, medication side effects. Sometimes the missing piece is behavioral: a functional behavior assessment and a plan that teaches replacement skills and reduces triggers. Sometimes the missing piece is environmental: the home routine is unintentionally setting off daily overload. You don't have to guess alone.

The empowered mindset shift that changes everything

Here is the shift that turns helplessness into leadership; **aggression is information. Safety is the priority. Skills are the solution.**

Information considerations: What is the chain? What is the trigger? What is the trap? Safety considerations: Reduce harm immediately, with calm authority. Skills-related considerations: Replace aggression with communication and regulation that actually work. This is how you stop living as a hostage to the next incident. When taking one of these approaches you become the architect of a safer system.

Closing: what I want you to remember about me after a hard day

After an aggressive episode, you may look at me and feel heartbreak mixed with fear. You might wonder if you're raising someone who will always be unsafe. **Please don't let your worst day become my identity.** Hold the truth with both hands: you can take aggression seriously without turning me into a monster. You can enforce boundaries without stripping me of dignity. You can build a safer home without breaking my spirit. When I'm aggressive, I'm not telling you I'm evil. I'm telling you I'm overwhelmed, unskilled, trapped, or terrified—and my body is using the only exit it knows.

Teach me a better exit. Build me a safer runway. Hold the boundary with calm authority. And when the storm passes, help me practice how to come back. That's how you protect our family *and* my future.

Chapter 5: Siblings in the Shadows

The silent cost of autism—and how you protect the whole family without leaving anyone behind

If you could see our family the way I see it, you'd notice something most people miss. You'd see the obvious part first: me—your autistic child—taking up the oxygen in the room when things get hard. The appointments. The IEP meetings. The therapy calendar. The emergency phone calls. The constant mental math you do every day—what will set me off, what will calm me down, what can we attempt, what should we avoid, how do we survive this week without another incident. But then you'd see the quieter part. The part that doesn't scream.

You'd see my brother or sister watching from the edge of the frame. They're there for it all. They hear the shouting. They feel the tension. They notice the way plans change around my needs. They notice which conversations happen behind closed doors. They learn the mood of the house like a weather system—reading facial expressions, listening for door sounds, counting how long it's been since the last meltdown, predicting whether today is going to be "good" or "dangerous." They love me. And sometimes they resent me while other times they fear me. And sometimes they feel guilty for all of it. **Because they're not the one with the diagnosis, they often become the invisible ones—the siblings in the shadows**.

This chapter is not here to make you feel like you're failing. It's here to give you power. There's a truth you deserve to hold without shame and it is this; when autism enters a family, it doesn't just change the child who is diagnosed. It changes every child. And if you want your home to stabilize, you can't treat siblings like background characters in a story that revolves around me. You don't need perfection. You need balance and structure supported by honest language. You need protection—for them and for you.

The sibling experience you don't hear about at school meetings

Siblings are often asked to mature too early. They become experts in swallowing disappointment. They become skilled at being "easy." They learn not to add to your stress, because they can feel how close you are to the edge. Some of them become protectors. They step between me and a fragile object. They try to calm me. They usher a friend out of the house quickly when things shift. They become little adults in a home that forces adulthood on everyone.

Some become silent. They retreat to their room, to their phone, to their own world—not because they don't care, but because caring hurts too much when it feels like it never changes. Some become loud and act out. They compete. They may even start breaking rules not because they're "bad," but because negative attention feels better than invisible attention.

And almost all of them carry a private question they don't want to say out loud:

"Do I matter too?"

If you only take one thing from this chapter, let it be this: your other children are not just "fine" because they get good grades, don't melt down, or don't require meetings. A child can look fine and still be carrying a heavy load.

The hidden costs: what siblings actually pay

There are five costs that show up in many autism households, even the loving ones.

The first is fear. Not fear in a dramatic way—fear in a quiet, internal way. The kind of fear that makes a child listen for footsteps, tense up when voices rise, avoid inviting friends over, or sit at the dinner table ready to run if the mood shifts. If my meltdowns have ever involved aggression, yelling, or destruction, siblings can become hypervigilant without anyone realizing it.

The second is role reversal. Your "typical" child becomes the helper, the mediator, the responsible one. On the surface, it looks like maturity. Underneath, it can be grief—because part of their childhood is being traded for stability.

The third is loss. Not always big losses, but a long string of small ones: the birthday party that had to end early, the restaurant you never go to anymore, the vacation that got canceled, the sports game you missed because I had a crisis, the family photo that became a battlefield. Over time, those small losses can build a quiet story in a sibling's heart: "My needs are optional."

The fourth is resentment and guilt. This is a particularly cruel pairing. They resent the attention I get, then feel guilty because they "know I can't help it." They resent you for being absent, then feel guilty because they know you're doing your best. They resent themselves for having normal wants.

The fifth is identity strain. Some siblings decide they must always be the "easy one." Others decide they must always be the "strong one." Some define themselves as the overlooked one. These roles can shape their personality long after childhood, especially if nobody names what's happening.

None of this means siblings are doomed. It means they need something specific from you—something you can absolutely provide.

What siblings need most is not equal—it's intentional

Parents sometimes hear "don't forget the siblings" and think it means dividing everything perfectly in half: equal time, equal attention, equal money, equal energy. That's not realistic. It's also not what siblings actually need. They need intentionality. For you to look them in the eye and communicate—through words and routines—that they are not an afterthought. That their emotional safety matters as much as my behavioral plan. And perhaps that their childhood is not collateral damage.

That begins with one powerful practice: **validation**. Not minimizing. Not spinning it into positivity or correcting their feelings. Simply naming the truth.

"I know that was scary."
"I know you missed out today, and it wasn't fair."
"I see how much you've been carrying."
"You can love your sibling and still feel mad sometimes."
"I can handle your honest feelings."

When siblings hear that, something in them loosens. They stop feeling like they have to pretend. When siblings don't have to pretend, homes get calmer—because the emotional pressure isn't building silently in every corner.

Your safety plan can't only be for the autistic child

When we have incidents of **maladaptive aggression**—hitting, biting, throwing, chasing, breaking objects—our family needs a safety plan that protects everyone without shaming anyone. The plan doesn't need to be complicated; it just needs to be consistent. It helps to think of it as a fire drill. Not because I am a fire, but because everyone deserves to know what to do under unexpected stressful moments. A solid sibling safety plan includes three elements:

A safe place.

A room, a neighbor's house, a locked bathroom, a specific spot outside—somewhere siblings can go that is predictable and protected.

A simple signal.

A word or phrase that means, "Move now." Not shouted in panic, but spoken with calm authority. My siblings should know that when they hear it, there's no debate and no delay.

A job for each person.

Not a job that makes siblings responsible for me—but a job that helps them feel empowered. One sibling grabs their phone and goes to the safe place. Another takes the dog. Another locks the door. The point is to reduce chaos, not to make them parent. One mother described using a color system—green, yellow, red—so everyone understood the level of escalation without long explanations. When their autistic son went "red," siblings knew exactly where to go. The plan didn't erase meltdowns, but it removed the terror of uncertainty. It gave siblings power instead of fear. Safety plans don't make your home feel like a hospital. They make it feel like leadership exists, even when things get hard.

The ritual that heals siblings more than any speech

Siblings don't just need protection from scary moments. They need proof that they are still cherished. There is one practice that changes sibling outcomes more reliably than almost anything else: **predictable, protected time**. Not big vacations. Not occasional gifts. Not once-a-year apologies after a hard season. Time that is small, consistent, and undivided. Fifteen minutes can be enough if it is real. No phone. No multitasking. No checking on my noise in the next room. Just you and them.

A teenage sister once said that she felt like she didn't exist for years. Then her father started taking her for weekly coffee dates—nothing fancy, just a simple ritual. She didn't say it made everything perfect. She said it made her feel seen again. That's the point.

Siblings aren't asking you to stop caring about me. They're asking you not to disappear from their lives while you care for me. If your schedule is chaos, make the ritual smaller. A walk around the block. A bedtime check-in. A quick ice cream run. A weekly "choose the music" drive. Something repeatable. Something that belongs to them. Predictable time becomes an emotional anchor. It tells a sibling, "Even in a hard family, I still have a place."

Protect their identity like it's a fragile treasure

One of the quiet tragedies in autism families is when siblings begin to define themselves only through autism. They become the helper, the peacemaker, the easy one, the forgotten one, the "mature one." And then they grow up and struggle to know what they actually like, want, or need.

You can prevent this by doing one simple thing on purpose: **protect the sibling's separate life.** Protect their sports, their music, their friendships and their hobbies. Their celebrations and their milestones. Not in a perfect way but in a consistent way. Sometimes that means you split coverage—one parent takes the sibling to the game while the other stays with me. Sometimes it means you recruit support—grandparents, trusted friends, paid help, community resources—so the sibling doesn't lose their whole childhood to the family's crisis cycle. If you can't protect everything, protect one thing. One recurring event that signals: "Your life matters." When siblings have their own identity, they don't have to compete with autism and they don't have to resent me to find themselves. They can love me without losing themselves.

How to talk to siblings about autism without turning it into a burden

Many parents avoid conversations because they don't want siblings to feel responsible. But silence creates its own burden—kids fill the gaps with assumptions. The healthiest approach is honest, age-appropriate truth. Tell them autism affects my nervous system. Tell them I can feel overwhelmed in ways that look extreme. Tell them aggression is never okay, and you are building skills and safety. Tell them they can always come to you with their real feelings, even the messy ones. **Most importantly, remind them of this: "You are not responsible for fixing your sibling."**

That sentence needs to be said out loud sometimes—especially to the child who naturally becomes the helper. Siblings should be invited into compassion, not drafted into caretaking.

A home can't heal if every relationship is strained

Parents often focus on the autistic child—and rightly, because the needs can be intense. But siblings are part of the emotional ecosystem of the home. When siblings are unseen, resentment grows. When resentment grows, the home becomes tense. When the home becomes tense, my nervous system becomes more reactive and then the cycle tightens.

So supporting siblings isn't a side project. It's a stabilization strategy. When siblings feel safe and valued, the whole family breathes differently. I benefit too—not because siblings become my therapists, but because the emotional climate becomes less fragile.

The future question siblings are afraid to ask

As siblings get older, another weight can creep in: the future. "Will I have to take care of my sibling when my parents are gone?" Even if you haven't said it, they may fear it. And fear thrives in silence. You don't need to solve the entire future in one conversation. But you can reduce fear by naming what you are planning. At age-appropriate levels, let siblings know there is a long-term plan. Tell them they will be included, not obligated. Tell them you are thinking about services, supports, legal planning, living arrangements, community resources—whatever fits your reality. When siblings know there is a plan, they relax. When they don't, they often carry a silent dread that shapes their entire adolescence.

Closing reflection: bring the siblings back into the light

I know you didn't choose this. I know you didn't imagine parenting would include fear drills and crisis management and constant adaptation. I know you're tired. But if you can bring siblings out of the shadows—if you can validate them, protect them, give them a safety plan, and give them predictable time—you will change the trajectory of your whole household.

Your autistic child will still have needs. There will still be storms. But the family won't fracture quietly around the edges.

Siblings are not supporting actors. They are children with hearts that notice everything. See them. Name their reality. Keep them safe. Give them a place that is theirs. And when you do, you won't just preserve your family—you'll strengthen it. Because they're not the one with the diagnosis, they often become the invisible ones—the siblings in the shadows.

Chapter 6 — If I Run, I'm Not Being Bad—I'm Escaping

Elopement is my emergency exit—build layers of prevention, not punishment.

What Elopement Really Is

There are moments you can feel before they happen. You might see it in my eyes—the way my focus slips away, the way my face tightens like a door closing. Or you notice it in my body: my hands start picking at fabric, my feet begin to bounce, my breathing turns shallow, my movements get sharp. You say my name once, then twice, and try to redirect me with logic, reminders, consequences. But by then, I'm not weighing obedience against disobedience. I'm weighing whether my body can survive what it's experiencing. And when I run—when I bolt, slip away, vanish down an aisle, dart across a parking lot, push through a doorway, disappear into the neighborhood—I need you to understand the truth with no ambiguity: **I'm not running from you; I'm running from overwhelm.**

That's elopement in plain language. It isn't daydream wandering. It isn't a child "testing" you. For many autistic children, **it's a nervous-system emergency**—an escape response where the body chooses flight because staying feels unbearable. The tragedy is that the nervous system is trying to save me, but the world I run into can hurt or kill me. Cars don't know I'm overloaded. Water doesn't care that I'm panicking. Heights don't pause because my impulse is stronger than my judgment. Strangers don't automatically understand that I'm not a "bad kid," I'm a dysregulated child whose brain has shifted into survival mode. If you've ever chased a child through a parking lot with your heart hammering, you already know this is not a "behavior problem" in the ordinary sense. It's a safety problem, and it's urgent.

To respond well, you have to understand what running usually means inside an autistic nervous system. Most people assume motive: defiance, rebellion, manipulation, a desire to scare the parent, a desire to "win." But **elopement is often a wordless coping mechanism that is communicating:** *This is too much and I can't stay here*. Sometimes it's driven by discomfort or pain—constipation, reflux, headaches, ear infections, fatigue—that a child can't explain clearly, so their body tries to change the environment. Sometimes it's sensory overload: lights feel sharp, noise feels like pressure, crowds feel like collision, smells feel like invasion, clothing feels like a trap. A store that looks ordinary to you can feel like standing too close to a concert speaker, except I can't step away and everyone keeps talking. Sometimes it's demand overload—transitions stacking up, instructions chaining together, a "quick errand" becoming an unpredictable maze of waiting and stimulation, a task like hygiene or homework feeling impossible because it's too many steps, too much shame, too much pressure. Sometimes it's also the pull toward something that feels regulating or predictable: a familiar route, the quiet of outside air, the certainty of home. And sometimes it's an impulse under stress—the part of the brain that pauses, plans, and considers consequences goes offline, and the body simply moves.

This is why punishment so often fails in the moment. If you treat elopement like a moral problem, you miss what it actually is: a communication problem and a regulation problem that can become a life-or-death problem in seconds. **When my nervous system hits red alert, I'm not available for a lesson. I'm looking for an exit.**

Prevention Beats Reaction: Build Layers That Hold

The most important mindset shift is simple—prevention beats reaction—because if you only respond once I'm already running, you will spend your life in fear. Instead of asking, "How do I stop this?" The better question becomes, "What conditions make running more likely, and how do we lower those conditions before we hit the danger point?" Elopement rarely yields to a single fix because when a nervous system is in flight, one weak barrier will break. **The families who stabilize don't rely on one strategy; they build layers**, like you would around a pool: supervision, barriers, alarms, skills, and rules. Elopement requires the same kind of safety engineering.

One layer is the environment. You make exits harder to slip through and easier to monitor, not because you distrust your child, but because you respect how fast impulse can outrun judgment. Parents sometimes feel guilty about alarms or extra locks, as if safety measures mean imprisonment but safety structures are seatbelts. They don't erase freedom; they prevent tragedy, and they also protect you from living in constant hypervigilance.

Another layer is lowering triggers that push the nervous system toward flight. Elopement is often patterned, even when it looks random, and it tends to cluster around certain times of day, certain environments, certain transitions, certain demands, or certain sensory loads. When families track it gently—without blame—they often discover predictable pressure points: after-school collapse, loud bathrooms, crowded stores, the chaos of morning routines, the shame spiral around homework or getting dressed, the friction of unexpected change. **Lowering triggers doesn't mean lowering expectations forever**; it means lowering pressure while you teach new skills, and redesigning routines to fit the nervous system you are parenting rather than the one you wish existed. Sometimes the most powerful prevention is unglamorous: food before errands, fewer errands in a row, shorter trips, clearer transition warnings, headphones in loud places, less talking during escalation, more recovery time after school, and predictable exit plans that aren't running.

A third layer is replacement—because if running is my best coping tool, I will keep using it. You don't only block elopement; you teach me a safer way to accomplish the same purpose: relief, distance, regulation, control. And because language often drops under stress, the replacement has to be simple enough to use when my brain is overloaded. Many families teach a break routine that functions like a life skill, not a reward: a safe phrase, a safe space, and a practiced sequence that leads to calm. The key is trust. In the beginning, that break routine has to work reliably, because if I signal "break" and you say, "No, finish first," my nervous system learns the new exit is fake, and it will keep reaching for the one exit that always works. Once the skill is established, you can shape it—two minutes of break, then one small step—but first you install the pathway and prove it's real.

When Danger Spikes: Respond, Recover, and Reduce Repeat Events

Even with prevention and replacement, there will be moments when my body still tries to bolt, and those moments can make your heart feel like it's leaving your chest. This is where parents accidentally escalate the situation by chasing and yelling, because panic makes the body loud and fast. But a child in flight can interpret loudness and speed as a threat, even when you're trying to save them, and that can push them to run harder or into more danger. In acute elopement, you're not trying to "win compliance." You're trying to prevent catastrophe. The most effective response tends to be calm authority, fewer words, and physical positioning that blocks danger without turning the moment into a fight—getting between the child and the road, moving toward the safest containment point, using consistent short cues that always mean the same thing.

Some children don't only run; they climb, jump, dart into streets, move toward water, or scale balconies and furniture with frightening determination. Parents often experience these as dangerous self-induced events—moments where the child's body moves faster than the parent's ability to predict. These episodes can be driven by sensory seeking, impulse under stress, escape at any cost, or a mismatch between physical ability and safety awareness. Whatever the reason, the response remains the same: treat it like a safety engineering problem, not a character problem. You stop asking, "Why would they do that?" and start asking, "How do we make this harder to do and easier to interrupt while we build safer skills?" **That may mean modifying routines, removing access points, increasing supervision in risk zones, and taking the environment seriously—not as punishment, but as protection while the nervous system learns alternatives.**

Hope is essential, but hope without a plan creates panic, so families who face elopement need an emergency routine that is practiced, not imagined. If your child disappears, you don't want to invent your first steps while your hands are shaking. **You want a simple, rehearsed sequence**: where to look first, who calls, how tasks divide if two adults are present, how siblings move to safety, and what information you'll provide quickly if help is needed. Identification strategies can also be part of safety—whatever fits your child's dignity and tolerance—because when minutes matter, clarity matters. Some families build a small network of trusted neighbors or caregivers who understand that a bolting child may not respond typically, because familiarity can prevent a situation from turning dangerous or misunderstood.

When the event ends—when you find me, when we get back inside, when adrenaline drops and anger surges—this is the moment that shapes what happens next. If the home becomes a courtroom, I can associate returning with shame and threat. If the event is ignored completely, the brain can file elopement under "effective coping strategy." But if you respond with calm structure, you can protect safety and teach skill without breaking trust. Repair does not need a long lecture; it often works best as a short reset, followed later—when calm is real—by practicing the replacement pathway again. The nervous system learns from repetition, and what you practice after the storm is what becomes available before the next one.

Closing reflection

Elopement can make you feel powerless in a way few parenting challenges do, because it forces you to confront the truth that love alone doesn't stop a body in flight. If you've ever felt judged in public, if you've ever blamed yourself in private, if you've ever gone to bed replaying the "what if" outcomes you narrowly avoided, I want you to hear this clearly: responding to elopement is not about proving you're a strong parent. It's about becoming a prepared parent. Prepared parents don't rely on hope or harshness; they build systems. They stop treating running as a personal offense and start treating it as a signal that the nervous system is past capacity. They install layers that hold, they teach an exit that is safe, and they practice a plan so fear doesn't lead the decisions.

And here's the most important part: the goal is not just to stop me from running today. The goal is to help me learn—over months, over years—that I can feel overwhelmed and still be safe, that I can ask for relief without risking my life, and that the people who love me will protect me without turning my fear into shame. When you do that, you're not only preventing a dangerous moment. You're building a future where my nervous system doesn't need the street, the parking lot, the water, or the unknown to find air. You're building a home where safety is real, calm is possible, and escape is no longer the only language my body knows.

Part III: My Autism Lives Inside a Whole Family.

Chapter 7: My Siblings Love Me… and They Get Hurt Too

Protect my childhood while protecting me—without making anyone the villain.

The Story You Don't Always See From the Outside

My siblings can love me deeply and still feel bruised by life with me. Both truths can live in the same house at the same time. They can be proud of me one minute and furious the next. They can defend me at school and then collapse in tears at home. They can understand—at least intellectually—that my brain works differently, and still feel like their own needs keep getting pushed to the edge of the family's attention. When people talk about autism in families, they often talk about parents and the autistic child, as if everyone else is just "supporting cast." But siblings aren't in the supporting cast. They're children growing up inside the same storm, trying to build their own nervous system and identity while the household revolves around crises, schedules, therapies, and unpredictability.

Sometimes their hurt is loud. It shows up as anger, sarcasm, fighting, defiance, withdrawal, jealousy, or suddenly "acting out" in ways they never did before. Sometimes it's quiet. It shows up as being too good, too helpful, too invisible. It shows up as a child who stops asking for things because they've learned the answer is usually "not right now." It shows up as a child who becomes hyper-responsible, who monitors your mood, who tries to prevent my meltdowns before you even notice the early signs—because they've learned that the house can flip fast. When siblings live in an environment where unpredictability is normal, many of them grow up reading the emotional weather the way sailors read waves. They learn to anticipate. They learn to adapt. And they often pay for those skills later with anxiety, perfectionism, guilt, or a quiet resentment they don't know how to name.

The most painful part for them is that their hurt can come with shame. They may feel guilty for being angry at me. Guilty for wishing things were different. Guilty for wanting more attention. Guilty for thinking, even for a moment, "Why does everything have to be about him?" So they bury it. Or they project it. Or they turn it inward. And when they turn it inward, they may start believing a secret story: *My needs matter less.* Even if you never say that out loud, family dynamics can unintentionally teach it when every day is triage.

From the inside of the autistic child, I want you to know something important: I don't want to steal their childhood. I don't want to be the reason they feel invisible. I don't want to be the reason you feel like you're constantly choosing who to protect. But autism doesn't ask for permission. It demands attention. It escalates at inconvenient times. It turns ordinary moments into emergencies. And if our family doesn't build intentional protection for siblings, they can become collateral damage in a war they never volunteered for.

How Siblings Get Hurt—and How Families Accidentally Make It Worse

Siblings get hurt in obvious ways and subtle ones. The obvious ones are easier to name: being hit, scratched, screamed at, having toys broken, being interrupted mid-sentence because my needs escalate, having plans canceled because the day becomes unsafe. When aggression or meltdowns happen, siblings may feel physically unsafe in their own home, which is one of the most destabilizing experiences a child can have. A home is supposed to be the place where you relax your nervous system. If a sibling is always bracing—always listening for the sound that signals escalation—they don't truly rest. They survive. And survival mode has a long memory.

The subtle injuries can be harder to notice because siblings often don't complain in clear language. They experience chronic "micro-losses": the birthday party that gets cut short, the family dinner that ends with yelling, the vacation that becomes a series of containment strategies instead of joy, the parent who is emotionally unavailable because they're exhausted, the sibling who learns they can't bring friends over, the sibling who becomes the "easy child" because being easy feels like the only way to be loved without adding to the load. These micro-losses add up to a sense that family life is always controlled by the highest need in the room, and if the sibling is not the highest need, they disappear.

Families accidentally make it worse when they treat siblings' pain as something to manage rather than something to honor. Sometimes parents, exhausted and defensive, say things like, "You know your brother can't help it," or "You need to be patient," or "You're older, so be the bigger person." Those sentences are often true in a narrow way, but they can land like a quiet dismissal: *Your hurt isn't allowed here.* Siblings can interpret that as, *My feelings are inconvenient.* And when feelings become inconvenient, kids stop sharing them. That is where distance starts.

Another way families accidentally worsen the sibling experience is by turning them into junior therapists or junior parents. It happens without anyone intending it. A sibling becomes the translator, the helper, the co-regulator, the one who distracts me so you can cook dinner, the one who watches me for five minutes "just while I run upstairs," the one who gives up their room, their quiet, their preferences, because "it's easier" than fighting the meltdown. Over time, a sibling can become a silent employee of the household, and the cost is that they don't get to simply be a child. They may become competent, sure—but competence isn't the same as being cared for. In fact, competent siblings are often the ones nobody checks on because they don't cause trouble.

Some siblings also carry a fear they can't name: fear that my needs will always come first, fear that the family will never be normal, fear that their own future will be tied to mine, fear that one day they will be expected to become my caregiver. That fear can show up as avoidance, as anger, or as a refusal to engage with anything related to autism. If you interpret that refusal as "selfish," you miss the truth: sometimes it's the only way a child knows how to protect their own emotional boundaries when the family system feels overwhelming.

And here is the part many parents don't want to admit because it's painful: siblings can begin to resent not just me, but you. Not because you are bad parents. Because they see you as the gatekeeper of attention and fairness, and when fairness feels broken long enough, resentment looks for a target. If you don't make space for siblings to be angry *safely*, that anger will find an unsafe place to go—outbursts, acting out, depression, or a slow emotional retreat from the family.

Protecting Everyone Without Making Anyone the Villain

A healthy family doesn't require siblings to love autism. It requires siblings to feel safe, seen, and protected while living alongside it. That's the goal: not perfection, not constant harmony, but safety and belonging for everyone in the system.

Protection begins with something simple that changes everything: you name the sibling experience out loud. Not in a lecture. In a steady, respectful acknowledgement that gives them permission to tell the truth. "I see that this is hard." "I see that you get interrupted." "I see that sometimes you don't feel safe." "I know you love your sibling and also feel hurt." When you say those sentences, you give siblings a rare gift: emotional legitimacy. You remove the shame that tells them they're wrong for having complicated feelings. And once they feel legitimate, they're more likely to talk instead of acting it out.

Then you build two kinds of safety: physical and emotional. Physical safety means siblings aren't expected to "just tolerate" aggression. If my behavior can become dangerous, the family needs clear rules about space, supervision, and protection. That doesn't mean harshness toward me. It means realism. It means creating routines where siblings know what to do when escalation starts, where they can move to a safe zone, where they are not trapped in close quarters during high-risk moments. Emotional safety means siblings are not punished for expressing fear or frustration, and they are not turned into caretakers of your feelings. They should never feel responsible for keeping the house calm. They should never feel like their truth will break you.

One of the strongest tools for sibling protection is something parents often resist because it feels unfair: protected time that belongs to the sibling. Time that is not canceled unless the house is truly on fire. Time where they get a parent's undivided attention, even if it's short. Ten minutes of fully present connection can do more for a sibling's nervous system than an entire day of distracted proximity. The point isn't the length; it's the certainty. It tells them: *You still have a place here that isn't negotiable.*

Another powerful tool is "separation without shame." Many families assume siblings must always be together because that's what a "close family" looks like. But sometimes siblings need distance to recover. They need their own activities, their own friends, their own space, their own quiet. Giving siblings separation isn't rejecting the autistic child. It's protecting the sibling's development and mental health. And when siblings feel their boundaries are respected, they're more likely—ironically—to be warm and connected when they are together. Forced togetherness breeds resentment. Supported distance can rebuild compassion.

You can also protect the sibling relationship by creating a shared language in the house. Not clinical language—human language. "He's overloaded." "She's in the red zone." "We need space." "We're going to reset." When siblings have words for what's happening, the chaos becomes less personal. They stop thinking, *He's doing this to me,* and start thinking, *His nervous system is overwhelmed.* That shift doesn't erase hurt, but it reduces the feeling of being targeted.

There's a final layer that matters more than almost anything: **permission for siblings to have their own story**. They are not required to be inspirational. They are not required to be endlessly patient. They are not required to become mini-advocates. Some siblings will grow into fierce protectors; some will need distance; some will oscillate. Your job isn't to control their feelings. **Your job is to create a family culture where love is not measured by how much pain they can tolerate.**

Because here is the truth I wish I could say clearly when I'm dysregulated: I want my siblings to feel safe with me. I want them to feel proud of me without feeling trapped by me. And I want you to stop living as if you must choose between protecting me and protecting them. You can do both—but it takes intention, structure, and a willingness to honor everyone's reality, not just the loudest crisis.

Closing reflection

Siblings are often the quiet heroes of autism families, but **"hero" is a dangerous label for a child**. It can hide pain and reward self-erasure. It can make a sibling feel like their worth comes from how much they sacrifice. So if you want to protect your family long-term, don't ask siblings to be heroes. Ask the family system to be fair. Fair doesn't mean equal attention every day. It means every child knows they are seen. Every child knows they are protected. Every child knows their feelings have a place. Every child knows the house will not ask them to carry burdens meant for adults.

If you can build that kind of fairness—through safety plans, protected sibling time, permission to have complicated feelings, and boundaries that prevent siblings from becoming caretakers—you will not only reduce resentment. You will preserve relationships. You will give siblings the chance to love me without losing themselves. And you will give me the chance to grow up not as the villain of the family story, but as a child who is both protected and accountable inside a home that refuses to sacrifice one childhood to save another.

Chapter 8: I Can Feel Your Marriage Straining

Stress turns partners into coworkers—here's how to stay united when life is on fire.

When Love Turns into Logistics

I notice it long before you say it out loud. It's in the way your voices change toward each other when you're tired—shorter, sharper, more transactional. It's in the way your eyes meet less often, like there isn't enough room in the day for softness anymore. It's in the way you talk to each other only about schedules, school calls, therapy sessions, medication refills, who's picking up, who's dropping off, who's covering the meltdown risk at the grocery store. You're not arguing about love. You're arguing about load. And when a family is under constant pressure, load is what turns two partners into two exhausted coworkers sharing a household.

Autism can strain a marriage not because parents don't care, but because the work is relentless and unpredictable. Our home can feel like a command center: manage triggers, prevent elopement, respond to aggression, negotiate the school system, protect siblings, keep food on the table, keep your jobs afloat, keep your nervous systems from snapping. When you live like that for long enough, romance doesn't die from a single blow. It dies from a thousand small disappearances—moments when you would have reached for each other, but instead you reach for the next task. Moments when you would have laughed, but instead you're bracing for the next incident. Moments when intimacy could have happened, but your body is too tense to be touched.

And then there's the cruelest part: you can still love each other and still feel like you're losing each other. You can still be loyal and still feel lonely. You can still be committed and still feel like you're parenting in parallel instead of partnering together. Many couples don't break because they stop caring. They break because stress keeps them in survival mode for so long that there's no oxygen left for connection.

If you've felt that shift, you're not imagining it. The strain is real. But it's also workable—if you stop treating marriage as something that will "come back" later, and start treating it as part of the family system that must be protected now.

The Patterns That Pull You Apart—and the Small Moves That Pull You Back Together

Stress doesn't just create tension; it creates predictable patterns. One of the most common is a silent division of roles: one parent becomes the crisis responder, the one who can de-escalate, the one who knows the protocols, the one who absorbs the hardest moments. The other parent becomes the stabilizer—income, logistics, errands, bills, keeping the "outside life" from collapsing. Sometimes these roles are chosen. Often they happen by accident. And when they harden, both parents start feeling unseen. The crisis parent feels trapped—like they're carrying the emotional weight alone. The stabilizer feels blamed—like they can't do anything right because they weren't the one in the room when the crisis happened. Resentment grows quietly from both sides.

Another pattern is what I call "the scoreboard." It's the mental tally that builds when you're exhausted: who got up last night, who took the day off work, who missed the meeting, who handled the meltdown, who never gets a break, who always does bedtime, who carries the paperwork, who gets more sleep. The scoreboard isn't evil—it's a sign that fairness is breaking down and nobody feels protected. But if you live by it, you stop being a team. You become competitors for rest. In that state, even small misunderstandings can ignite because you're not fighting about the dishes or the late pickup; you're fighting about whether life is evenly crushing you.

Then there's the pattern of "different grief speeds." Parents don't process autism the same way, and they don't process it on the same timeline. One parent may accept quickly and move into problem-solving. The other may stay in grief longer—still mourning what they thought life would be. One may read every book and want every therapy. The other may feel flooded and want less talk and more quiet. One may be more emotionally expressive; the other may shut down. None of these differences are wrong, but under stress they can look like betrayal: "Why don't you care as much as I do?" or "Why are you always talking about this?" or "Why can't you just help?" When grief speeds differ, couples misinterpret each other's coping style as character.

The way back starts with one core principle: **you don't need perfect agreement—you need shared leadership**. Shared leadership means you stop operating like two separate managers and start operating like one unit with two bodies. **The easiest way to do that is to create one protected space each week where you talk about the system, not the mistakes**. Not a long therapy session. Not a blame session. A short "family ops" meeting that is calm, scheduled, and designed to prevent resentment from building in silence. You talk about what's working, what's not, where the next pressure points are, what support you need, and what trade-offs you're making on purpose instead of by accident.

What makes this work is the tone: *the meeting isn't a courtroom. It's an engineering review. You are redesigning a high-stress system together.* When couples frame it that way, a subtle shift happens. They stop asking, "Why aren't you doing more?" and start asking, "How do we make this week survivable without burning either of us down?" That question alone can save marriages because it turns the relationship back into a team.

From there, you protect the marriage with tiny, repeatable acts instead of waiting for a grand romantic reset. Under intense caregiving demands, the mistake couples make is believing intimacy requires time they don't have. The truth is that **connection often requires consistency more than time**. A ten-minute check-in after bedtime, a hand squeeze during a hard moment, a "thank you" that is specific, a brief hug that isn't interrupted, a text that says "I see you," a habit of sitting together for five minutes before you scatter into tasks—these are not cute gestures. They are nervous-system medicine. They remind both adults, "We are still us." In a house that feels like a fire station, tiny rituals are how you keep the relationship from becoming only a work partnership.

You also need one hard boundary that protects the bond: no fighting in the peak of crisis. When a child is escalating, when you're dealing with aggression or elopement risk or a school emergency, your bodies are in threat mode. Threat mode is not a place for relationship truth. It's a place for survival. Couples often say things in those moments that are less about truth and more about adrenaline. If you can agree on a simple rule—"We don't solve marriage issues during a child crisis; we stabilize first and revisit later"—you prevent damage that takes days to repair. The goal is not to suppress conflict; it's to keep conflict from detonating when everyone's nervous system is already on fire.

Staying United in the Fire: Protect Roles, Restore Tenderness, Get Help Early

There's a reason autism strains marriages: it forces couples to confront limits they didn't know they had. It also forces them to renegotiate life in ways that can feel unfair. So unity isn't just an emotion you hope returns. Unity is a structure you build.

One of the strongest structures is role clarity without role imprisonment. You can divide responsibilities, but you don't lock them permanently. If one parent becomes the "behavior expert" and the other becomes the "money and logistics parent," you create dependence and distance. Over time, one parent feels trapped in the hardest moments while the other feels excluded, and both resent it. Instead, you build cross-training. Even if one parent is naturally better at de-escalation, the other learns the basics. Even if one parent is naturally better at logistics, the other learns enough to step in. Cross-training doesn't mean equal skill. It means shared competence, so neither parent feels alone and neither parent feels like a bystander in their own family.

Another structure is protected rest. **Marriages don't fracture only from conflict; they fracture from exhaustion**. If neither parent ever truly rests, tenderness becomes impossible because the body is always bracing. You don't need luxury rest; you need scheduled relief that is respected like medication. That may look like one parent getting a guaranteed hour off on Tuesday nights while the other covers, and then switching on Thursdays. It may look like a Saturday morning rotation. It may look like bringing in help—family, respite, paid support—so the marriage is not forced to carry every hour alone. Couples who survive learn that asking for help is not weakness; it is a strategy to protect the relationship that holds the whole family.

And because this chapter is written from the inside of the child, I want to say something that many parents don't allow themselves to hear: when your marriage collapses, I feel it. Even if you don't fight in front of me. Even if you keep your voices low. Even if you think you're hiding it, I feel the distance. I feel the tension. I feel the coldness. I feel the way the house tightens. **It can make my nervous system more reactive because instability in the adults becomes instability in the environment.** That's not your fault; it's just how sensitive systems work. When your partnership is stable, the whole home becomes safer for me—even if my symptoms don't change overnight.

So please don't wait until you're at the cliff edge to take the marriage seriously. If you're already in constant conflict, if resentment is thick, if intimacy is gone, if you can't speak without fighting, get support early. Not because you're failing, but because **the load you're carrying is big enough to require reinforcement**. Some couples need counseling. Some need a parent coach. Some need behavioral support so home life becomes less explosive. Others need a financial plan so panic stops driving everything. The point isn't the specific service, rather it is this: you don't keep carrying a burning house alone and then act surprised when you're collapsing. You call in reinforcements.

Closing reflection

When life is on fire, it's easy to believe marriage is something you'll return to later—after the diagnosis settles, after therapy starts working, or after the next crisis ends. But "later" can become a mirage in autism parenting because needs don't always decrease on schedule. If you want to stay united, you can't treat your partnership as an optional luxury. It's part of the foundation that keeps our family standing.

You don't have to become perfect communicators. You don't have to force romance when you're exhausted, and *you don't have to pretend you're fine*. What you do need is a few strong commitments that hold under pressure: to stop keeping score and speak about load instead of blame while meeting weekly and redesigning the system together to protect tiny rituals of connection. To cross-train so no one is trapped in one role forever, and to ask for help before resentment becomes the language of your home. That is how you stay partners instead of coworkers. That is how you keep love alive inside the logistics. And that is how you show me—your autistic child—that even under intense strain, family can remain a place of unity, not fracture.

Chapter 9: I Changed Your Career – and I Know You Miss Yourself

I didn't mean to take your future hostage. But I know my needs rewrote your days—and I see what it cost you.

The Moment Work Stopped Being Simple

I know there was a version of your life where you could leave the house without doing a risk assessment first. Where your phone ringing didn't instantly spike your heart rate. Where you could say yes to a meeting, a trip, a late dinner, a presentation, a promotion—without quietly calculating what it would do to our home. Then autism entered the room, and the rules changed.

It didn't always happen dramatically. Sometimes it started as "just a few appointments," a few early pickups, a few difficult mornings. But you know how it goes. Therapy schedules multiply. School calls become a weekly rhythm. A child who looks "fine" to outsiders melts down the moment the day demands too much. You start needing more flexibility than your workplace can tolerate, and you start needing more predictability than life will give. You begin saying no—not because you stopped caring about your career, but because someone had to keep the household from tipping over.

And here's the part nobody tells you: career change in an autism household is rarely a single decision. It's often a slow surrender by inches. You miss a networking event because we had a rough day. You turn down the travel role because routines are fragile. You stop volunteering for high-visibility projects because you can't promise availability. You start choosing "less exposure" over "more opportunity" because every additional demand at work can ripple into a crisis at home. Eventually, you look up and realize you're no longer building the future you imagined—you're maintaining stability like it's your full-time job.

You didn't choose that because you're weak. You chose it because you're responsible and because you know what happens when a family runs out of stability. You've lived the nights when no one slept, the mornings when the school called before you even finished coffee and the stretches where your nervous system stayed on high alert for so long that you forgot what calm felt like. People on the outside will label your career shift like it's "just priorities," as if you casually swapped ambition for caregiving. But inside our house, it didn't feel casual. It felt like the ground moving under your feet.

The Grief Nobody Gives You Permission to Name

I can feel it when you miss yourself. Not in the dramatic way people imagine grief—crying on the floor, falling apart every day. Sometimes it's quieter than that. Sometimes it looks like you going through the motions, handling everything, still performing competence, still getting things done—while a part of you is dimming in the background. It shows up in the way you talk about the old version of your work like it belonged to someone else. It shows up when you see other people's career updates and feel something tighten in your chest. It shows up in the way you hesitate before answering the question, "So what do you do?" because what you do now isn't what you trained for, planned for, or dreamed of.

You can love me fiercely and still feel the loss of your own trajectory. Those truths can exist in the same body at the same time. You don't have to pretend you're fine just because you're grateful. You don't have to silence grief just because you love your child. Love doesn't erase loss—it carries it. Sometimes the grief is about money, because financial pressure becomes a constant hum in the background of everything. You do the math in your head: therapies, supports, missed work, reduced hours, lost promotions, one income instead of two, savings that don't grow the way they should. Sometimes the grief is about status, the quiet dignity of being excellent at something the world recognizes. Sometimes it's about identity: the feeling that your adult self got swallowed by schedules and crises and advocacy. And sometimes it's about freedom—simple freedom—like being able to take a breath without thinking, *What's going to happen at home if I'm gone too long?*

I want to say something to you that you might not expect from the voice of the child: **you are allowed to miss yourself without feeling guilty**. That guilt doesn't protect me; it just drains you. And when you are drained, everything in the system becomes more fragile—your patience, your marriage, your health, your capacity to lead during storms.

I've seen this happen in families. A parent who was once confident and alive becomes a crisis manager who never gets to be off-duty. They stop doing the things that used to restore them because restoration feels selfish when there's always something urgent. They tell themselves, "When things calm down, I'll get back to me." But autism seasons can stretch. "When" can become a moving target. And if you wait for the perfect calm, you may wake up years later wondering where your life went. Here's the truth: *you don't lose yourself in one day. You lose yourself by delaying your return to yourself again and again.*

How You Rebuild a Life Without Abandoning Me

Rebuilding doesn't mean you pretend this didn't change you. It means you stop letting it erase you. The first step is not a big career leap. It's permission. **Permission to treat your identity as essential infrastructure, not as a luxury item you earn after you've solved everything**. In an autism household, you can't wait to "finish the work" before you take care of the adults, because the work doesn't finish in neat chapters. So you build a life that includes you while you're still parenting in the fire.

That usually starts with something small and consistent—something that belongs to you and is protected the way you'd protect my therapy appointment. It might be a weekly block of time where you do meaningful work even if it's not your old job title. It might be a certification you keep alive. It might be a professional community you stay connected to so you don't disappear or a creative thread—writing, teaching, building, designing—anything that reminds your nervous system. *I still exist as a person, not only as a caretaker.* The size doesn't matter at first. The repeatability matters. When you practice returning to yourself, you become less resentful, more resilient, and more capable of leading me through hard moments.

Then comes redesign—what you do for money and meaning may need to change shape. For many parents, the breakthrough isn't finding "the perfect job." **It's building a work model that matches the unpredictable reality of our home.** Sometimes that means remote work. Sometimes it means consulting. Sometimes it means project-based roles instead of high-travel leadership tracks. Or it may even mean entrepreneurship, not because you want to gamble but because you need better control over your schedule. It may even mean a season of reduced output with the explicit plan to ramp back up later—an intentional pause, not a silent disappearance.

We once met with a Mother in this scenario—brilliant, trained, ambitious—who thought leaving her high-status role would break her. Instead, what broke her was trying to keep it while carrying a constant crisis at home. When she finally shifted into a smaller consulting practice, she didn't become less capable. She became more stable. She worked fewer hours, but her hours had integrity. She had room to breathe. She reclaimed pieces of herself she hadn't felt in years. *It wasn't the career she originally imagined, but it was a career she could actually sustain—and that sustainability improved the whole family.*

A father in another family didn't want to "step back," because stepping back felt like losing. But he was constantly torn between work demands and school emergencies, and the friction was eating his marriage alive. He negotiated a role change—less visibility, more flexibility—and at first he felt bruised by it. Later, he admitted something that surprised even him: *the shame faded when the home stopped feeling like a daily emergency.* He still had ambition. He just stopped paying for it with constant household collapse. In time, as the family stabilized he rebuilt upward again from a steadier base. What these families have in common is not luck. It's design. **They stopped treating the situation like a personal failing and started treating it like a system that needed engineering: how do we stabilize income, protect identity, and reduce crisis load all at once?**

There's another piece you can't skip: shared load. If you have a partner, the career impact can't quietly land on one person forever without consequences. Even when one parent becomes the "career anchor" and the other becomes the "care anchor," that arrangement has to be intentional, revisited, and rotated when possible. Otherwise, one parent's identity erodes while the other parent's pressure explodes, and both end up resentful. This isn't about being perfectly equal. It's about being consciously fair, and about refusing to let one adult disappear for the system to function.

And finally, you build support—not because you're incapable, but because you're human. When families don't have support, they use the most expensive support available: the total sacrifice of a parent's identity, health, and future. Even modest support can buy back hours, and hours are everything. Hours become rest, become work. Hours become therapy follow-through and marriage repair. Hours become patience. In homes like ours hours are not a matter of convenience. They are survival currency.

Closing reflection

If you've felt like your career got hijacked, like your ambition had to shrink to keep our home from breaking, like the old version of you is fading in the rearview mirror—I want you to hear this in the clearest voice I can give you: **I see you. I see the version of you that shows up even when you're tired**, the version of you that adapts even when you didn't ask for this life, the version of you that keeps the lights on and the household moving with a strength most people will never understand. But I also want you to know something that matters just as much: I don't need you to disappear for me to be loved. I need you to remain steady. I need you to feel resourced. I need you whole enough to lead when my nervous system is on fire. Reinforcing your identity is not a betrayal of caregiving—it's part of what makes caregiving sustainable.

You can grieve what changed without drowning in it. You can rebuild without waiting for a perfect calm. You can return to yourself in small, consistent ways that add up over time. And when you do, you're not choosing your career over your child. You're choosing a future where our family doesn't survive on sacrifice alone—where it survives on design, support, and a kind of love that includes you too.

Part IV: The Future Is Heavy in Your Chest.

Chapter 10: People Think I'm Naughty. You Feel Judged. I Feel Unsafe.

Public shame fuels private burnout—use scripts, exits, and boundaries that protect dignity

What They See, What You Feel, What I'm Actually Living

When we walk into the world together, three different realities show up at the same time.

The first is what *they* see. They see a child who won't sit still, who shouts, who covers their ears, who melts down in an aisle, who refuses to move, who hits or throws or runs. They see a moment stripped of context: no sleepless night before, no sensory overload, no anxious brain, no communication struggle, no twelve earlier "almost-meltdowns" I barely held together. They see five minutes and decide they know my character—and your competence.

The second is what *you* feel. You feel the looks before I even explode. You know the way heads turn when my voice gets loud. You know the way someone raises their eyebrows as if they've caught you failing. You see the parent with the calm child and feel the comparison hit like a bruise. Your heart splits its attention: half on me, trying to keep me safe; half on them, bracing for the silent verdict. You love me fiercely, but in those moments, love doesn't erase the shame that creeps in, because you're human, not a robot. You're wired to register rejection, and public parenting with an autistic child can feel like standing under a spotlight with no script.

The third is what *I'm* actually living. I'm not thinking, "How can I embarrass you?" I'm thinking something more primitive without words: *Too much. Too loud. Too bright. Too fast. Too many rules. Too many eyes. Too much change. I don't know how to make this stop.* My body floods with signals I don't know how to regulate. My brain is trying to process lights, sounds, smells, people, your words, my feelings, and invisible rules about how I "should" act. When it all collides, I don't feel naughty. I feel unsafe. And when you tense up because you feel judged, my body feels that too, and now I'm not only overwhelmed by the environment—I'm overwhelmed by the fear of losing you emotionally in that moment. From the outside, it looks like defiance. On the inside, it feels like drowning.

Public life is where these three realities collide: their misreading, your shame, my panic. If that collision happens often enough, it doesn't just make errands hard. It feeds something deeper—what you might call advocacy burnout. *You're not only fighting systems in meetings and on paper; you're fighting the "system" of public opinion every time we leave the house.* The battles at school and with insurance are draining enough. Add strangers' judgment on top, and even a short grocery run can feel like another IEP war—only with no table, no agenda, no allies, and no exit plan. When that becomes the norm, something in you begins to close. You avoid outings. You say no to invitations. You shrink your life to the spaces that feel safer, not because you don't want to live, but because you're tired of bleeding in public.

I'm not asking you to stop feeling that pain. I'm asking you to recognize what's really happening: the world mislabels me as naughty, then mislabels you as incompetent, and both labels are lies. The more you can see that clearly, the less power their confusion has over your nervous system—and the more capacity you have to help my nervous system feel safe again.

How Public Shame Turns Into Private Burnout

Every public incident leaves a trace. You may think it's just another hard day, another meltdown at Target, another restaurant visit cut short, another sideways glance at the playground. But your body keeps a score that your mind doesn't always read. Each time you feel judged, a little more tension takes up permanent residence in your muscles. Each time you rush out of a store with a crying child, a small part of you files the world under *danger*. Each time someone makes a comment, even a subtle one, your brain adds it to the evidence list that says, *See? It's not safe out here.*

Over time, that evidence list becomes heavy. It sits next to the paperwork stack, the IEP files, the appeal letters, the medical summaries, the behavioral plans. You don't only advocate in meetings. You advocate every time you enter a room and silently ask the world, *Please let my child exist here without being shamed.*

Public shame becomes private burnout because it multiplies the number of fronts you're fighting on. You're not just trying to secure services and interventions; you're trying to defend your child's right to be seen as human. That means you're always "on," always ready to explain, always deciding whether to educate or ignore, always carrying a layer of armor over your skin. Even when nothing goes wrong, you're bracing for the moment it might.

That bracing has a cost. It leaks into places that should feel like refuge—your home, your marriage, your sleep. You wake up already tired because your nervous system never truly comes off duty. You start saying no to things you once loved because you don't have the social energy for another round of managing other people's reactions. You may even start snapping more at me or at siblings—not because you've stopped loving us, but because your stress bucket is full and public life keeps tipping more into it. There's another layer: the internalized story. Even if you know intellectually that my behavior is rooted in regulation, not morality, judgment can creep in sideways. After enough public incidents, it's easy to hear a subtle whisper: *If I were a better parent, this wouldn't happen so often. If I were more consistent, more patient, more organized, better at routines, better at therapy homework—maybe we wouldn't be here.* Shame doesn't need strangers once it gets inside. It can replay their voices using your own.

That's how burnout tightens its grip. It's no longer just, "I'm tired of these situations." It becomes, "I'm tired of who I'm forced to be in these situations." You start to feel like parenting me in public requires a version of yourself you can't sustain—part security guard, part crisis manager, part public relations specialist, part educator, part apologist. Here's the truth you need to hear: you don't need to be all those things. You need to be my parent. And parents lead best when they have tools, exits, and boundaries that protect everyone's dignity—including their own.

Scripts, Exits, and Boundaries That Protect Dignity

When life is on fire in public, you don't need a philosophy—you need something you can actually *do* in the moment. Think of three kinds of tools as your core kit: scripts to reduce decision load, exits to reclaim safety, and boundaries to stop handing your nervous system to strangers.

Scripts are pre-chosen words you can lean on when your brain is flooded. *They're not about winning arguments; they're about reducing your cognitive load so you can stay centered.* **A good script is short, honest, and repeatable.** It might sound like, "He's autistic—this is sensory overload. We're handling it." Or, "She has a disability and is overwhelmed. We're doing our best." Or simply, "We're having a hard moment. Thanks for giving us space." You don't have to explain our whole story. You don't have to prove your parenting. You are offering enough context to deflect attack without inviting a debate. And if speaking feels impossible at that moment, your script might even be silent—a small card you keep in your wallet, a practiced nod, a hand gesture to signal "We're okay, but not available." *The point is not perfection; the point is that you're not inventing language while trying to hold me together.*

Exits are not failures. They are safety valves. **You're allowed to leave before the meltdown peaks.** You're allowed to step outside, to sit in the car, to abort the mission entirely. You're allowed to decide that protecting our nervous systems matters more than finishing the shopping list or sitting through the entire dinner. Where burnout grows is in the belief that you *must* stay to prove something—to your family, to strangers, to yourself. When you treat leaving as leadership instead of defeat, you give yourself permission to protect us from unnecessary harm. Over time, you can design exits that are more graceful—quiet checks at the door, "preview visits" to build tolerance, short trips with planned breaks—but at the beginning, the most important thing is this: you never owe the world your meltdown to be considered strong.

Boundaries are how you stop giving away your sense of worth to anyone who happens to be watching. A boundary might be internal: *I will not interpret stares as evidence that I am failing.* It might be relational: *I will not engage with strangers who are clearly judging rather than asking.* It might be practical: *I only explain our situation to people who speak with respect.* Boundaries are not walls against love; they are filters against harm. When you chose them ahead of time, you reduce the number of decisions you have to make under stress. You don't stand in the cereal aisle trying to decide whether to educate the person glaring at you. You already decided yesterday: ***I save explanations for people who are worth the energy.***

Dignity is the thread that runs through all of this. You are not just managing behavior; you are modeling how a human being responds when misunderstood. When you move with calm authority—using simple scripts, choosing exits without shame, and holding boundaries that say, "My worth and my child's worth are not up for public vote"—you teach me something much deeper than how to stand in line. **You teach me how to exist in a world that may never fully understand me.**

You may worry that using scripts and exits is "giving in." It isn't. It's strategic. It conserves your energy for the advocacy battles that matter most and keeps you from burning all your fuel on every disapproving glance. It keeps you whole enough to keep showing up for the long haul instead of collapsing from constant, unnecessary fights.

Closing reflection

People will think I'm naughty. Some of them will think you're weak. Some of them will think our family is chaotic, broken, "too much." You can't control that. You can't educate every stranger, win every opinion, or turn every public moment into a victory. What you *can* do is decide whose voices reach your heart, and how you will move through the world with me anyway.

Public shame will always try to become a private story. It will try to convince you that their misunderstanding is your truth. **But your truth is this: you are raising a child whose nervous system is wired differently in a world not built for that difference. That is hard. That is holy.** That is work most people will never have the courage to do. You don't owe perfection to anyone watching. You owe presence to the child who is holding your hand.

When you use scripts that lighten your mental load, exits that prioritize our safety over appearances, and boundaries that keep strangers out of your self-worth, you're not only protecting yourself from burnout. You're building a model I will carry inside me long after this chapter of childhood ends. *You're showing me that being misunderstood doesn't have to mean being ashamed,* that hard moments don't cancel our right to be in public, and that dignity is something we can protect even when life is messy.

I will remember less of what the strangers looked like and more of how you stood beside me.

If what I remember is a parent who stayed grounded, who chose us over their image, who didn't let the world's confusion turn into our shame—that will be one of the greatest gifts you ever give me.

Chapter 11: Friends Disappear. I Notice.

Isolation isn't your imagination—rebuild community with people who can handle our reality.

When the Circle Gets Smaller

I notice when the invitations stop coming. I may not understand every social rule, but I feel the absence. I feel it when the phone doesn't ring anymore, when playdates quietly evaporate, when birthdays are celebrated without us, when conversations trail off after you say my name and explain my needs. I feel it when you hesitate before reaching out to someone you used to trust, already preparing yourself for the polite distance that might follow.

You notice it too, even if you don't say it out loud. One by one, people fade. Some leave because they don't understand autism. Some leave because our life is unpredictable and uncomfortable. Some leave because they offered help once, didn't know what to do, and felt awkward coming back. And some leave because they simply don't have the capacity to sit with complexity when it stops being theoretical.

What hurts most isn't always the loss of the people themselves—it's the message that can creep in quietly: *We are on our own now.* That message changes how you move through the world. You stop asking. You stop expecting. You start carrying everything yourselves, because relying on others has become too risky emotionally. It's easier to be exhausted than disappointed again.

From the inside of the child, I want you to know this: when friends disappear, I don't assume they're busy. I assume I'm the reason. Even if you never say it, children are excellent pattern detectors. I see how your world shrinks around me, and I can feel the weight you carry trying not to resent that fact. That's a heavy burden for both of us.

Why Parents Resist Respite—Even When They're Drowning

This is usually the moment when someone says to you, "You need a break." And this is usually the moment when something in you hardens.

Respite sounds reasonable on the surface, but emotionally it can feel like surrender. It can feel like admitting you can't handle your own child. It can feel like failure. For some parents, it even feels like abandonment—as if stepping away means you're betraying the one person who needs you most. And if you've already lost friends, already feel isolated, the idea of handing my care to someone else can feel terrifying. *What if they don't understand me? What if they do it wrong? What if I melt down? What if I feel unsafe? What if you feel guilty the entire time anyway?*

So you do what strong, loving parents often do: you push through. You tell yourself you'll rest later. You convince yourself that you're fine, that this is just what parenting looks like now. **You become incredibly capable—and dangerously depleted**.

But there's a truth hidden under all that resistance, and it's one most parents only admit after they're already burned out: **doing everything alone doesn't make you a better parent. It just makes you tired**. And tired parents don't have more love to give; they have less margin. Less patience. Less resilience. Less ability to repair when things go wrong. I feel that too. I feel it when your fuse is shorter than you want it to be. I feel it when your body is present but your spirit is worn thin. I feel it when siblings get less of you because there simply isn't anything left to give. Resisting respite doesn't protect me from harm—it quietly spreads the harm across the whole family.

What Respite Actually Does—for You and for Me

Respite is not a statement about your love. It's a strategy for survival. When parents take breaks—real breaks, even short ones—something important happens. Your nervous system resets. Your body remembers what calm feels like. You come back more patient, more grounded, more emotionally available. Marriages soften when there is space to breathe together, even briefly. Siblings get moments of undivided attention that remind them they still matter as individuals. And the home becomes less brittle, less likely to shatter under the next stressor.

There's another truth that often surprises parents: **I benefit from respite too.** When it's done thoughtfully and gradually, respite teaches me flexibility. It shows me that other adults can be safe. It helps me practice coping in small, supported doses. It expands my world instead of shrinking it. I don't need you every second to feel loved—I need you regulated enough to lead me well.

I know the fear that lives in your chest when you imagine leaving me with someone else. That fear is real. But so is the cost of never leaving. Parents who finally try respite often describe the same experience: the first time is terrifying, emotional, and awkward. And then—slowly—they realize they've been running on fumes for years. They realize they forgot what silence feels like. What uninterrupted thought feels like. What being a partner instead of a crisis manager feels like. They don't come back weaker, they come back steadier and steadiness is what helps me most.

Respite doesn't have to look one specific way. Sometimes it's in-home, with someone who comes into our space so routines stay familiar. Sometimes it's out-of-home, in a structured program designed for kids like me. Sometimes it's community-based—faith groups, nonprofits, autism-friendly programs. And sometimes it's informal: another family who understands, a relative who learns my cues, a quiet rotation of care that makes life possible for everyone involved. The form matters less than the function. **The function is relief.**

Closing reflection

When friends disappear, it can feel like the world has quietly decided you're too much to deal with. It can make you cling tighter, work harder, and carry more than any one family should. But isolation is not strength, and exhaustion is not devotion. Respite doesn't mean you're weak. It means you're wise. It means you understand that no one thrives without air. Every parent needs space to breathe. Every marriage needs time to reconnect. Every sibling needs moments where they are not competing with crises. And every child benefits from parents who are not permanently depleted.

I don't measure your love by how long you stay without rest. I feel your love in how you return—calmer, clearer, more yourself. Respite is not abandonment. It is love with foresight. It is how you survive this journey, and how our family can do more than endure. It is how we keep our world from shrinking—and slowly, carefully, let it open again.

Chapter 12: School Meetings Make You Fight. I Just Want to Belong

Turn IEP battles into a plan that actually works for my brain—and our family's peace.

What Happens in Those Rooms That Changes Us

I can feel it before you even sit down. Your shoulders tighten. Your voices drop into a careful, controlled tone. You start gathering papers like armor—IEPs, evaluations, progress reports, emails you printed "just in case." By the time you walk into the conference room, you're no longer just my parents. You're negotiators. Defenders. Translators. And sometimes, adversaries—not only to the system, but to each other.

School meetings are strange like that. They rarely feel collaborative, even when everyone says the right words. The table is full of adults, but somehow the person the meeting is about—me—feels furthest away. You're talking about goals, accommodations, behavior plans, data points, incidents. You're trying to be calm, reasonable, informed. But underneath all of it is something rawer: fear. Fear that I'll be misunderstood. Fear that I'll be labeled difficult. Fear that I'll be managed instead of known. Fear that if you don't fight hard enough, I'll disappear into a system that was never designed for me. And this is where the strain begins. Because you don't always fight the same way.

One of you may lean toward diplomacy—choosing words carefully, trying to keep the relationship with the school intact, worried that too much pushback will backfire on me later. The other may feel the urgency differently—every missed accommodation feels like a threat, every vague answer feels like dismissal, every delay feels like neglect. One of you wants to de-escalate. The other wants to escalate. And suddenly, the meeting doesn't just expose the school's limitations—it exposes the fault lines in your partnership.

You leave those rooms exhausted, not only because advocacy is draining, but because you've had to hold two roles at once: united parents on the outside, divided processors on the inside. By the time you get back to the car, the fight isn't about the IEP anymore. It's about tone and about who spoke up. About who stayed quiet and whether you looked "too aggressive" or "not aggressive enough." Meanwhile, I'm still the same child who walked into school that morning just wanting to feel like I belong somewhere.

When Advocacy Becomes a Relationship Stressor

School advocacy has a way of sneaking into every corner of family life. It follows you home. It shows up at dinner and it interrupts sleep. It hijacks conversations that were supposed to be about anything else. And over time, it can quietly turn your relationship into a pressure cooker—because the stakes feel impossibly high, and the margin for error feels nonexistent. What makes this especially hard is that both of you are usually right in different ways. The parent who wants to maintain rapport with the school isn't weak; they're thinking long-term, worried about retaliation, burnout, or being labeled "that family." The parent who wants to push harder isn't unreasonable; they're responding to the daily reality of my struggles and the cost of delays that look small on paper but loom large in real life. You're not fighting because you don't care. You're fighting because you care in slightly different languages.

The system doesn't help. Schools often frame meetings as collaborative, but the power imbalance is real. Timelines move slowly. Language stays vague with promises that are conditional. Decisions get deferred and because you know I only get one childhood, waiting feels dangerous. So advocacy becomes relentless. You're always preparing for the next meeting, the next email, the next justification for why I need what I need. That constant vigilance can make you sharp with each other, because there's no space to rest.

From my side of this, what I feel isn't the policy debate—it's the tension. **I feel it when school becomes a battleground in our home.** I feel it when my name triggers an argument and I also feel it when you talk about me like a problem to be solved instead of a person trying to survive a system that overwhelms me. Even when you think I'm not listening, my nervous system is. When the adults who are supposed to be my safe base are strained, school starts to feel even less safe—because now it's not just hard there; it's hard everywhere.

Here's the quiet truth: when advocacy turns parents against each other, nobody wins. Not the school. Not the marriage. And not the child who just wants to feel like they're more than a case file.

Shifting the Focus: From Winning Meetings to Building Belonging

What I need most from school is not a perfect plan on paper. What I need is a sense of belonging. Belonging doesn't mean every day is easy or that accommodations magically fix everything. It means I'm seen as a whole person, not a disruption to manage. The way you advocate can either move us closer to that—or pull us further away.

That starts with a shift in how you approach meetings together. Before you walk into the room, you decide something important: you are on the same side, even if your styles differ. **Advocacy is not a test of who is right; it's a strategy problem you solve as a unit.** When you talk beforehand—about priorities, red lines, and roles—you reduce the chance that frustration will spill sideways onto each other. One of you might take the lead speaking. The other might take the lead observing and note-taking. These roles aren't about hierarchy; they're about preventing overload and miscommunication.

It also helps to narrow the focus. Schools often overwhelm families with too many goals, too many metrics, too many "areas to address." But I don't experience my day in bullet points—I experience it in moments. Transitions. Noise. Social confusion. Unstructured time. Instead of fighting every battle at once, you choose the few changes that would most improve my daily sense of safety and dignity. When meetings center on *how I experience school*, not just how I perform, the conversation changes. Teachers are more likely to understand. And you're less likely to leave feeling like you failed because you didn't fix everything.

Another powerful shift is remembering that advocacy doesn't end at the table. *Sometimes the most meaningful work happens outside the meeting—building one genuine relationship with a teacher who wants to understand and empower me,* preparing me for what school will feel like tomorrow, or helping me recover after a hard day so school doesn't become associated only with pain. Those things don't show up in official minutes, but they shape my sense of belonging far more than perfect wording in a document. It's okay to acknowledge that school advocacy is one of the most marriage-straining parts of this journey. But when you process together instead of against each other, the pressure releases instead of accumulating.

Closing reflection

When school meetings make you fight, it's rarely because the relationship is broken. **It's because the system keeps asking you to defend something sacred—your child's right to belong—using tools that were never designed for love**. That kind of mismatch creates tension in even the strongest partnerships.

What I want you to remember, from the inside of the child you're advocating for, is this: I don't need you to win every meeting. I need you to remain steady. I need you aligned and I need to be assured that when school is confusing or painful, home is not another place where I become the source of conflict. When you walk into those rooms as a team, and you protect your relationship as fiercely as you protect my accommodations, you give me something no policy can guarantee—a sense that I am worth fighting for *without* tearing my family apart. School may always be imperfect for me. Meetings may always be exhausting. But if I can feel that you're united—that you're advocating not just for my performance, but for my belonging—then even in a flawed system, I have a place to stand.

Chapter 13: I Hear You Worry About When You're Gone

Make a future file that protects me—and gives you oxygen now

The Fear You Carry Quietly

You think I don't notice, but I do. I hear it in the way your voice drops when you talk about the future. I feel it in the pauses that stretch too long when someone asks, "What happens when he's older?" or "Have you thought about long-term plans?" I sense it late at night, when the house is finally quiet and your mind won't rest, because the question you don't want to ask out loud keeps circling: *What happens to my child when I'm gone?*

That fear doesn't come from a lack of faith in me. It comes from love mixed with responsibility. You know how much of my stability lives in your presence—your routines, your advocacy, your understanding of my signals, your ability to translate my world to others. **You worry that without you, I'll be misunderstood, mistreated, or lost in a system that doesn't see me as you do**. And because the thought is unbearable, you often do what humans do with unbearable thoughts: you push them away. But pushing it away doesn't actually give you peace. It just turns the fear into background noise—constant, draining, and heavy. It steals oxygen from your present because you're carrying an undefined future on your back. You may tell yourself, *I'll deal with that later,* but later never quite arrives, and the worry quietly compounds.

From inside the child you're raising, I want you to hear this: **thinking about my future without you is not a betrayal of me. It's an act of care**. And doing it intentionally doesn't make today darker—it actually makes today lighter.

What a "Future File" Really Is—and Why It Matters

A future file is not a morbid document. It's not a prediction of loss– a bridge. It's a way of transferring what you know, what you've learned the hard way, and what makes me *me* into something that can guide others when you're not there to explain.

Right now, you carry all of that information in your head and your body. You know my triggers, my comforts, my warning signs, my medical quirks, my sensory limits, my communication style, my strengths, my fears. You know which battles matter and which ones can be let go. You know how to tell the difference between a meltdown and a bad day, between defiance and overwhelm, between danger and distress. That knowledge is priceless—and fragile—because it lives mostly inside you.

A future file is how you protect that knowledge.

At its core, it's a living document that answers one simple question: *If someone else had to step in tomorrow, what would they need to know to keep my child safe, respected, and understood?* It doesn't have to be perfect. It doesn't have to be finished all at once. It just has to exist. When parents hear this, they often feel two things at once: relief and resistance. Relief, because part of them knows this would ease the constant low-grade panic. Resistance, because creating it feels emotionally heavy, and because it forces them to confront a future they'd rather not imagine. That resistance is human. But here's the quiet truth: **not having a plan doesn't protect you from that future—it just leaves you alone with it**. A future file is not about expecting the worst but about refusing to leave everything unspoken.

What Belongs in the File—and What It Gives Back to You

The power of a future file isn't in its format. It's in its clarity. It speaks when you can't. It advocates when you're tired. It carries your voice forward. At minimum, it holds three kinds of information.

The first is practical safety. This includes medical details, diagnoses, medications, allergies, providers, emergency protocols, and any behaviors that pose risk to me or others. Not in clinical language alone, but in real-world terms: what escalation looks like for *me*, what helps, what makes it worse, what never works. This is the information that keeps me physically safe and prevents unnecessary trauma when someone unfamiliar is in charge.

The second is relational truth. This is where many parents underestimate their importance. This section explains how I experience the world: how I communicate, what calms me, what frightens me, what respect looks like to me. It names my strengths—not as inspirational slogans, but as usable guidance. It explains how to build trust with me and how easily trust can be broken. This is the part that protects my dignity. It reminds future caregivers, educators, or guardians that I am not a checklist—I am a person.

The third is vision. This is where you get to say what you hope for me, even if you're not sure how it will all unfold. What kind of environment do I thrive in? What does a good life look like for *me*, not compared to anyone else? What values matter in decisions made on my behalf? Independence? Community? Safety? Joy? Routine? Growth at my pace? This section doesn't lock the future into one path, but it gives direction when choices must be made without you.

Creating this file does something unexpected for parents: it gives you back oxygen *now*. When your fears are undefined, they run wild. When they're named and structured, they shrink to a size you can carry. You stop mentally rehearsing catastrophic futures because you know you've left guidance. You stop feeling like everything depends on you never getting sick, never aging, never needing help. You haven't solved everything—but you've shifted from helplessness to leadership. And that shift matters. It changes how you show up today.

Closing reflection

I know the thought of a world without you is unbearable. It should be. You are my anchor, my interpreter, my advocate, my safe place. Nothing replaces that. Planning for my future without you does not mean you expect to disappear. It means you love me enough to prepare the ground beneath me, no matter what comes.

When you **create a future file**, you are not giving in to fear—you are taking authority over it. You are saying, *I will not let my worry steal all the joy from today.* You are choosing to live with more breath in your body, because you've done something concrete to protect me beyond your presence. One day, I may not understand every choice you made. But I will feel the result of this one. I will feel safer because you thought ahead. I will feel seen because you left words that explain me. And I will feel loved—not only because you stayed, but because you prepared.

You don't have to finish this in one sitting. You don't have to get it perfect. You just have to begin. And when you do, something subtle but powerful will happen: the future will loosen its grip on your throat, and the present will become a little more livable again—for both of us.

Chapter 14: Independence Isn't One Thing

My "independence" may be supported, shared, or staged—and it can still be a good life

The Word That Carries Too Much Weight

Independence is a word that follows you everywhere. It shows up in school goals, therapy reports, casual conversations, and late-night worries. People say it as if it means one clear thing: living alone, working full-time, managing everything without help, needing no one. When that version of independence feels uncertain for me, the word can land like a quiet verdict—*less than, behind, failing, not enough.*

I hear it when you lower your voice and ask professionals what they think is "realistic." I feel it when goals are framed as all-or-nothing, as if my life will either measure up or fall short. And I sense the grief that sneaks in when you compare me to a future you once imagined, one where independence looked simpler, cleaner, more recognizable to the world. But here is the truth I want you to hold gently and firmly at the same time: independence is not a single destination. It is not a fixed standard or a moral achievement. It is a relationship between a person and the supports that allow them to live with dignity, safety, and meaning.

For some people, independence looks like total self-sufficiency. For others, it looks like interdependence—knowing how to receive help and contribute within a system. For others still, it looks like staged independence—skills that are built, scaffolded, revisited, and adjusted over time as life changes. None of these are failures. They are human arrangements. The danger isn't that my independence might look different. The danger is letting a narrow definition of independence steal your ability to see the life that is possible for me, right now and in the future.

The Many Shapes a Good Life Can Take

When people talk about independence, they often confuse *support* with *limitation*. They assume that needing help means lacking agency, and that autonomy only counts if it's solitary. But many adults—neurotypical and neurodivergent alike—live supported lives without shame. They share homes. They rely on partners. They use assistants, tools, systems, and accommodations. They design lives that work instead of forcing themselves into lives that don't.

My independence may be supported. That might mean I live with family longer than expected, or in a setting where staff help with daily tasks, or in a community designed for shared responsibility. Support does not erase adulthood. It makes adulthood possible on terms that don't break me. When support is stable and respectful, it doesn't shrink me—it steadies me.

My independence may be shared. I may thrive in environments where roles overlap and contribution looks different. I might work part-time and contribute in ways that don't show up on a traditional résumé. I might bring consistency, focus, creativity, honesty, or care into spaces that value those things. A shared life does not mean a lesser life. It means a life built on connection instead of isolation.

My independence may be staged. I may master some skills early and others slowly. I may move forward, then step back, then forward again. I may need supports in one season and less in another. Progress may not be linear, and that does not invalidate it. Staged independence honors the reality that nervous systems develop at different rates, and that life circumstances change for everyone.

What matters most is not whether I check every box on a standardized list of adult milestones. **What matters is whether I can experience agency—having choices, preferences, voice, and influence over my own life**. Whether I can feel safe. Whether I can belong somewhere. Whether I can wake up most days without dread. Whether I can participate in the world in ways that don't constantly overwhelm my nervous system.

Those are the ingredients of a good life. And they are achievable in many forms.

How You Advocate Without Chasing the Wrong Finish Line

The pressure to chase a single version of independence can quietly distort decision-making. It can push families to prioritize appearances over sustainability, to rush skill-building without regard for burnout, or to frame every support as something to be "faded" as quickly as possible. When independence becomes a race, everyone loses.

A healthier approach begins with a different question: *What supports allow my child to function at their best without constant crisis?* From there, you build skills alongside supporters, not in opposition to them. You teach self-advocacy alongside assistance. You practice choice-making alongside structure. You introduce responsibility alongside safety nets. You measure progress not only by what I can do alone, but by how regulated, confident, and engaged I am while doing it.

This approach also protects you. When independence is defined flexibly, you stop feeling like every decision is a permanent verdict on my future. You allow room for experimentation, for growth, for course correction. You can say, "This works for now," without fearing that "for now" means "forever." You can plan for support without grieving them as proof of failure.

I want you to know something important: I do not need you to turn me into someone else to feel proud of me. **I need you to help me become more *me*, with the right support around me.** When you advocate for independence that fits my nervous system instead of fighting it, you reduce struggle and increase possibility.

Closing reflection

Independence isn't one thing, and it isn't a finish line you either cross or miss. It is a living arrangement between a person and the world around them. My independence may be supported, shared, or staged—and it can still hold dignity, contribution, and joy.

If you can release the idea that there is only one "right" outcome, you will find more peace in the present and more creativity in planning the future. You will stop measuring my life against someone else's blueprint and start designing a life that actually works for me. And in doing so, you will give both of us something precious: relief from the constant pressure to prove that we are enough.

I don't need a perfect version of independence. I need a sustainable one. A humane one. One that lets me belong, participate, and breathe. If you can hold that vision—steadily, without apology—you will not only protect my future. You will make space for a good life to unfold, one supported step at a time.

Part V: When Love Isn't Enough, Systems Must Change.

Chapter 15: My Needs Evolve as I Develop; Our Family Support System Should Too

Growth changes the child—and it must change the system around me

The mistake of freezing time

One of the most exhausting traps families fall into is believing that once a support plan is working, it should keep working. When something finally stabilizes—when meltdowns decrease, when school stops calling, when routines feel predictable—it's tempting to lock everything in place and hope nothing changes. Stability feels fragile, and the instinct is to protect it at all costs. But development doesn't freeze.

I am not the same child at seven that I was at four. I am not the same at twelve that I was at seven. My body changes. My brain reorganizes. My awareness grows. My social exposure increases. My tolerance shifts and what once soothed me may start to irritate me. What once overwhelmed me may become manageable. And what once felt impossible may suddenly feel boring—or humiliating. When the support system fails to evolve with me, it starts working *against* me.

Families often interpret this mismatch as regression. They worry something is going wrong. In reality, something is changing—and the system hasn't caught up. Support that was once protective can quietly become restrictive. Strategies that once reduced anxiety can begin to provoke it. Expectations that were once appropriate can suddenly feel infantilizing. And when that friction builds, behavior is often the first signal that something needs to be updated. Growth isn't the problem. Stagnant support is.

Development brings new stressors, not fewer

There's a myth that as autistic children get older, things naturally get easier. Sometimes skills increase, but the world also gets louder, faster, and less forgiving. Social expectations multiply and academic demands become less concrete. Independence is assumed before it is supported while emotional awareness sharpens without necessarily coming with better tools to manage it.

As I grow, I don't just carry my original sensitivities—I carry new ones. I become more aware of how different I am. I notice social hierarchies, sarcasm, rejection, and exclusion in ways I didn't before. I feel embarrassed and I feel the comparison. I even feel the weight of being watched and that internal complexity that often increases faster than my ability to regulate it. **If my support system is still built for the version of me that existed years ago, it will miss these shifts entirely.** This is where families feel blindsided. They think, *We already solved this.* But **development doesn't move in straight lines. It comes in waves** and each wave asks a new question: *Does this system still fit who I am now?*

When "working" support quietly stops working

There is a particular kind of frustration that arises when a child has outgrown their support, but no one has noticed yet. Sessions start feeling forced. Resistance increases. Cooperation drops. Parents hear phrases like "He's being oppositional" or "She's testing limits," when what's actually happening is misalignment.

Support that no longer fits often shows up as subtle signals before it explodes:

- Increased irritability around activities that used to be tolerated
- Withdrawal from supports that once felt neutral or helpful
- New anxiety that doesn't map to old triggers
- Shame or anger about being "treated like a little kid"
- Pushback that looks behavioral but is actually developmental

These moments are not failures. They are invitations to reassess. A healthy family system doesn't ask, *How do we get you back to who you were?* It asks, *Who are you becoming, and what do you need now?*

Support should mature as the child matures

As I develop, my support should become more collaborative, not more controlling. Less about compliance, more about agency. Less about external structure alone, more about internal skills—communication, self-advocacy, emotional literacy, and gradual independence with protection built in.

What helps at five is not what helps at ten. What stabilizes at ten is not what empowers at fifteen. At younger ages, support often centers on containment and predictability. As I grow, it should shift toward understanding and shared problem-solving. I need explanations, not just rules. I need to understand *why* things are happening, not just *what* is expected. I need opportunities to practice choice safely, to fail without being shamed, and to build identity without being reduced to a diagnosis. When support evolves with me, I don't feel managed. I feel partnered with.

The family system must evolve too

My development doesn't only change me—it changes the family ecosystem. Siblings grow and reinterpret the past. Parents age and carry cumulative stress. Marriages absorb years of adaptation. What worked for your family during early childhood may quietly erode during adolescence if it isn't revisited intentionally.

Families who thrive long-term don't just update therapy goals. They update roles, rhythms, expectations, and boundaries. They ask hard questions: *Who needs more protection right now? Who needs more autonomy? What are we holding onto out of fear rather than usefulness?* They also release guilt for needing different support at different stages. Needing more help later does not mean early interventions failed. It means development is unfolding.

Support is not a verdict on capability. It is a response to context.

Planning for evolution, not permanence

One of the most stabilizing things you can do as a parent is to expect change. Not fear it—expect it. When your family system is built with evolution in mind, transitions become less threatening. Reviews become routine instead of reactive. Adjustments feel normal instead of alarming.

This mindset changes how you approach help. You stop looking for a single solution that will last forever. You start building a flexible, layered support model that can scale, shift, and mature alongside me. That flexibility protects everyone from burnout and disappointment. Most importantly, it protects our relationship. When support grows with me instead of trapping me in the past, I don't have to fight the system to become myself.

Closing reflection

I am not static. Neither is autism. Neither is your family. If my needs seem to change faster than you expected, that doesn't mean you're losing ground. It means I'm developing. And development requires reassessment, not panic. Growth asks for curiosity, not control.

When you allow our support system to evolve—to become more precise, more respectful, more aligned with who I am becoming—you send a powerful message: *You are allowed to grow here.* You show me that support is not something I outgrow, but something that adapts as I do. Autism becomes a burden when the system around it is rigid. It becomes a strength when the system is intelligent.

If you keep updating the environment instead of blaming the child, if you keep designing support that fits the present instead of clinging to the past, you give me something invaluable: a path forward that honors who I am now—and who I am still becoming.

Chapter 16: If I Need Residential Care, I Still Need to Be Yours

Sometimes structure saves us—how to choose care without losing our connection

I can hear the fear even when you don't speak it. I feel it in the way your chest tightens when professionals mention "long-term placement." I notice how quickly you change the subject, how you reassure yourself that love and effort will somehow make every outcome different. And I understand why. For many parents, residential care feels like giving up, like choosing distance, like failing the most sacred promise you ever made. But I want you to hear this from inside the child you're protecting: if I ever need residential care, it doesn't mean I stop needing *you*. And it doesn't mean you stop being my family.

Residential care is one of the most misunderstood topics in autism parenting because it gets framed as abandonment instead of what it often is—an attempt to keep everyone safe, regulated, and alive when the needs of one person exceed what a single household can sustainably provide. Autism families already live in constant tension between love and capacity. Residential care sits right at that fault line. The truth you rarely get permission to say out loud is this: *sometimes the most loving choice is not the one that keeps everyone under the same roof, but the one that keeps the relationship intact.*

Separation Is Not the Same as Disappearance

When people imagine residential care, they often imagine a child being "sent away," visited rarely, managed by strangers, folded into an institution that erases individuality. That image is terrifying—and in some cases, historically accurate. But it is not the only reality, and it does not have to be *your* reality.

Residential care, when chosen thoughtfully and monitored fiercely, can be a form of *shared caregiving*, not replacement caregiving. It can be a setting where my daily regulation, safety, and skill-building are supported by trained professionals—while my emotional anchor remains you. I still need your voice, your presence and your advocacy. Your knowledge of who I am beneath my behaviors. I still need to know where I belong.

From my side, what hurts most is not physical distance. **What hurts is emotional disappearance. Being placed somewhere and slowly becoming invisible.** Being treated like a case instead of a person. Being talked about instead of talked with. Being "handled" without being known. That is the fear beneath your fear.

So let's be clear: if residential care is ever part of our story, what matters most is not *where* I live—it's whether I remain claimed. Whether I am visited, known, defended, celebrated, and remembered as someone who is still part of a family, not someone who was "too much" and quietly handed off. Children—and adults—can survive separation. *What they struggle to survive is disconnection.*

Choosing Care Without Surrendering Relationship

If residential care ever becomes necessary, it should be a decision made from clarity, not collapse. Too many families arrive there only after years of emergency—after injuries, constant crisis, sibling trauma, parental burnout, and fear that something irreversible is about to happen. In those moments, choices are rushed, guilt is overwhelming, and trust is thin. A different path exists.

Planning early—without committing to a single outcome—gives you power. It allows you to research environments that align with your values, to ask hard questions before you're desperate, to understand what "good care" actually looks like. Good care is not just about safety protocols and staffing ratios. It's about philosophy. About whether the environment sees autism as something to suppress or something to support. About whether families are welcomed as partners or treated as problems. And about whether residents are encouraged to build identity, routine, and purpose—not just compliance. If residential care is ever part of our future, your role does not shrink. It changes. You become the continuity and master translator. You become the long-term memory and the one who notices when something is off because you know me in ways no chart ever will. You become the person who ensures that care remains humane, individualized, and evolving as I grow.

And here is something parents don't hear often enough: choosing residential care does not erase your years of devotion, nor does it cancel your love. It doesn't undo the nights you stayed awake, the battles you fought, the systems you navigated, the parts of yourself you gave. Sometimes it is precisely *because* you have loved so fiercely that you recognize when a different structure is needed.

How to Choose Care Without Losing Me

Finding high-quality home and residential supports that honor dignity, safety, and family authority

If the day ever comes when you need outside care—whether that means intensive in-home support or a residential setting—**the most important decision you will make is not the facility itself, but the philosophy behind the care**. High-quality care is not defined by polished brochures or clinical language. It is defined by how deeply the provider understands *relationship*, *regulation*, and *respect*. Here is how you protect me while choosing help.

Start by prioritizing home-based care whenever possible. For many families, residential care becomes necessary not because the child cannot remain at home, but because the *right supports were never put in place early enough*. **The highest-quality providers work to stabilize the home first, layering skilled professionals into daily life so safety and regulation increase without emotional separation**. This approach preserves attachment, reduces trauma, and often delays—or completely prevents—the need for residential placement. At the top of any priority list should be providers who operate as extensions of your family, not replacements for it. When evaluating any provider—whether in-home or residential—use these non-negotiable filters.

First, **demand continuity of relationships**. High-quality care minimizes staff turnover, assigns consistent caregivers, and ensures that anyone working with me truly knows me—not just my behaviors, but my triggers, comforts, communication style, and strengths. Ask how caregivers are selected, trained, supervised, and retained. If the answer focuses only on credentials and not on relational stability, keep looking.

Second, **look for family-integrated care**, not family-excluded care. You should never feel like an outsider in decisions about my life. The best providers invite collaboration, welcome parental insight, and view you as essential partners. Whether it's BSP Solutions' concierge model or a residential program, the expectation should be clear: *you remain involved, informed, and influential.*

Third, **evaluate how regulation is prioritized over compliance**. Ask how the provider handles escalation, aggression, or elopement. Do they rely on control and punishment, or on nervous-system regulation and prevention? High-quality care understands that safety improves when stress is reduced—not when autonomy is stripped away.

Fourth, **assess dignity in daily living**. Observe how individuals are spoken to, how routines are explained, and how personal preferences are honored. Ask yourself: *Would I want to live here? Would I feel respected here?* If the answer is no, trust that instinct.

Finally, **plan proactively, not reactively**. The strongest families explore care options before a crisis forces a rushed decision. Even if you never use residential care, knowing your options reduces fear and gives you leverage. Choosing help does not mean you are stepping back. It means you are stepping up as a designer of your child's future. When you select care that aligns with your values, honors relationships, and keeps you involved, you ensure that—even if structures change—belonging does not.

Closing reflection

If the day ever comes when I need residential care, I don't need you to disappear in order for that care to work. I need you to stay connected. I need to know that I am still yours—not as a burden you handed off, but as a person you continue to choose.

You are allowed to hold two truths at once: that you would do anything for me, and that you cannot do *everything* alone. That tension does not make you weak. It makes you honest. If residential care ever becomes part of our story, let it be a chapter written with intention, oversight, and enduring relationship—not silence. Let it be a structure that supports life, not a line that divides it. And let me always know this, no matter where I sleep at night: I am still yours.

Chapter 17 — Find Out What I'm Built For

Follow my interests to unlock my "superpowers" - learning, confidence, and real sense of belonging.

There is a kind of light that turns on in a child that you can't coach, bargain, or force into existence. You can only recognize it when it appears. It looks like focus without strain. Curiosity that doesn't need rewards. Effort that doesn't require nagging. A spark that feels almost sacred because it's the opposite of the daily grind so many families live inside—appointments, interventions, school friction, social misunderstandings, meltdowns, shutdowns, and the quiet exhaustion of always trying to translate your child to the world.

When that light turns on, you're watching something more important than "engagement." You're seeing their identity begin to form. And for many autistic kids, that light tends to show up through something the world loves to label as a problem: **an intense interest.**

Oftentimes it shows up as a deep fascination. Or a hyper-focus - a world we return to again and again because it feels predictable, clean, and controllable in a world that often doesn't. It might be trains, weather, maps, animals, machines, numbers, space, coding, music, history, characters, languages, design, building, drawing—anything. The content matters less than the function. The interest is often my brain's way of saying, *"Here is a place I can breathe."*

Parents are frequently told to manage these interests the way you would manage an addiction—limit it, reduce it, redirect it, worry about it becoming "too much." And yes, sometimes the intensity can become rigid or consuming, especially when a child is stressed, anxious, overstimulated, or lacking other places where they feel competent. But the more profound truth is this:

Interests are not distractions. They are engines.

They are the most reliable doorway many neurodivergent kids have into learning, confidence, and real-world belonging—not the kind of belonging that requires them to perform a mask, but the kind that grows naturally from competence, contribution, and shared purpose.

I want to give you a different way to see your child's interests: not as a side quest to tolerate while you focus on "the real work," but as the bridge that turns the real work into something your child can actually carry. Because here's the uncomfortable reality most families eventually confront: **you can't build a life on correction. You can't build a self-image on constant remediation.** If most of your child's day is spent experiencing themselves as behind, wrong, too much, or not enough, you may see improvements in isolated skills—yet still watch their confidence slowly erode.

Confidence doesn't come from being told, "Good job." It comes from the experience of mastery. From the unmistakable moment when a child knows, *"I can do something that matters."* For many autistic kids, that moment arrives first through what they love. And when it does, something begins to reorganize inside them. You may see your child become more willing to try hard things in other areas—not because they suddenly got "more compliant," but because the world starts to feel less hostile. They have a place to stand. They have a home base. This is what I mean by the chapter title: **Find out what I'm built for.**

It's not a slogan. It's a developmental strategy. When a child discovers what they're built for, you're not just encouraging a hobby. You're giving them a way to meet the world without constantly feeling outmatched. **You're helping them build a stable identity** that can carry them through school, social discomfort, setbacks, and the weird emotional terrain of growing up. And you're doing something even more powerful: you're reframing the story. Instead of, "My child is hard," it starts to become, "My child is gifted in a way we are learning to harness." Instead of, "My child doesn't belong," it becomes, "My child belongs somewhere specific—and we're going to find it."

That word—*specific*—matters. Because one of the quiet cruelties of childhood is being told to belong everywhere. Neurodivergent kids often get punished for not fitting into broad, undefined social expectations. But belonging rarely works like that. Belonging is usually local. It happens in smaller rooms, around shared interests, in communities that have a common language. Belonging starts when your child finds "their people," not when they learn how to survive every crowd.

This is why interests can be so socially powerful. A child who struggles with small talk may come alive talking about engines, dinosaurs, robotics, music production, animation, weather systems, geography, or the history of ancient civilizations. An adult might hear that and think, *"He's monologuing again."* But if you listen differently, you realize the child is not trying to dominate. They're trying to connect the only way they know how—through depth. Depth, when guided well, becomes a bridge. It becomes a way to practice communication without shame. It becomes a way to practice reciprocity without forcing fake social scripts too early. It becomes a way to learn that conversation isn't only performance—it can be sharing. This doesn't happen automatically. It happens when parents learn to shape intensity into something portable. That is your role—not to crush the interest, but to convert it from a private island into a bridge that touches the world.

The simplest place to start is to watch what happens to your child's nervous system around their interest. Many autistic kids regulate through focus. Their body settles when they're immersed. Their anxiety drops. Their speech becomes more fluent. Their frustration tolerance improves. Their face changes. They look more like themselves. That calm state is not just "happy time." It's an opportunity. Because learning is easier when the nervous system is settled. Skill-building is easier when the child feels competent. Social risk is easier when the child doesn't feel exposed. So instead of asking, "How do I get my child away from this interest so we can do the real work?" ask a different question:

How do I use this interest to build capacity?

Capacity is the set of skills that make life work: attention, persistence, planning, communication, flexibility, emotional regulation, and confidence under stress. Interests can build all of them—if you choose the right moves. Here's what that looks like in real life.

A child who loves Legos isn't only building blocks. They are practicing sequencing, patience, fine motor planning, error correction, and resilience when something collapses and they rebuild. A child who loves maps isn't only memorizing cities. They are practicing pattern recognition, systems thinking, and storytelling ("If we go here, then here…"). A child who loves Roblox or Minecraft isn't only playing. They are practicing problem-solving, design, iteration, and sometimes collaboration. A child obsessed with weather patterns is practicing observation, prediction, and complex language—if you invite them to explain what they notice. A child who loves music production is building timing, emotional expression, auditory discrimination, and identity—often in a way that makes them feel powerful for the first time.

The magic isn't that the interest "fixes everything." The magic is that the interest gives you a platform for growth that doesn't feel like punishment. This is where many parents make a critical mistake: they see the interest, get excited, and then move too fast. They try to turn it into a full program, a business, a competition, a schedule, a new set of demands. The child rises for a while—then crashes. The interest becomes another performance arena. The spark dims. The child becomes guarded again. Your goal is not to commercialize your child's passion. Your goal is to protect it long enough for it to become a stable source of competence. Think of it like building a fire. If you smother it with too much wood too soon, it goes out. If you keep feeding it gradually, it becomes a steady flame that can warm the whole house.

This is also where parents often feel the fear beneath the surface: *What if this interest makes my child weird? What if it limits them? What if they become stuck?* It helps to understand something: when an interest becomes rigid, it's often not because the child is "choosing obsession." It's because the interest has become their safest place. If the rest of their day is full of confusion, criticism, sensory overload, or social pain, of course they will retreat into the one place that feels coherent.

So the solution is not to attack the interest. The solution is to widen the child's world so the interest isn't their only safe room. That widening can be gentle. It can be respectful. It can be done without war. One of the most effective strategies is to create what I call an "interest bridge"—a small expansion that stays close enough to feel safe. If your child loves trains, the bridge might be building a train station model. If they love animals, it might be drawing animal habitats. If they love weather, it might be tracking patterns and making predictions. If they love gaming, it might be learning one simple coding concept to modify a game or build a small one. The bridge doesn't pull them away from what they love; it gives their love a second room to live in. And over time, those rooms multiply.

That's how you build a life. At some point, a powerful shift becomes possible: contribution. This is where belonging starts to feel real—not because the child becomes more socially fluent overnight, but because the child becomes useful in a way that makes sense to them. A child who struggles with peer conversation may thrive when they get to show someone how something works. Teaching is structured. It has a purpose. It reduces the ambiguity that often makes social interaction painful.

When your child contributes—shows a sibling a build, explains a concept to a teacher, creates something another person enjoys—you're not just improving skills. You're repairing a narrative. You're giving your child evidence that they matter. And when a child has evidence they matter, they become more willing to risk connection. This is why "find what I'm built for" is not just about enrichment. It's one of the most strategic and compassionate ways to grow a child's confidence without forcing them to become someone else. Let me say it more plainly:

Many autistic kids don't need more pressure to be normal. They need more opportunities to be excellent in a way that is true to them. That excellence—whether it becomes a career, a skill, a craft, or simply a lifelong source of stability—creates the conditions where other growth becomes possible. Executive function improves when motivation exists. Language grows when a child wants to explain something. Social courage increases when the child has something to offer. Even emotional regulation becomes easier when life contains a source of predictable competence.

And for parents? This approach can heal you, too. Because the day-to-day grind of autism parenting can train you to look for problems. You become a scanner—always watching for the next meltdown, the next regression, the next complaint from school, the next social rupture. That vigilance is understandable. But it can also make the family story feel heavy.

Interests change the emotional tone of the home. They create moments of wonder. They remind you that your child is not a diagnosis walking around in pajamas. Your child is a person—with a mind that has its own architecture, its own beauty, its own kind of genius. By the end of this chapter, I want you to walk away with one truth planted firmly:

Your child's interest is a map.

Not a perfect map. Not the only map. But often the clearest one you're going to get. If you follow it with wisdom—protecting the spark, building capacity gently, expanding it through bridges, and creating opportunities for contribution—you give your child a path into learning, confidence, and belonging that feels earned, not forced.

What to do this week

Choose one interest your child returns to repeatedly, especially when they're tired or stressed. Don't judge it. Just observe it with respect. Then, create one small "build moment" around it—something they can complete and feel proud of in under an hour. After they finish, invite them to share it with you for two minutes. Not a performance. A sharing. Ask one question that signals genuine curiosity: "What part of this do you like the most?" or "What's the coolest thing about it?"

Finally, look for one doorway into community—not a crowded social arena, but a space where shared interest does the heavy lifting. A club, a lesson, a maker space, a workshop, a coach, a small group, a moderated online community. You're not shopping for friends. You're building the conditions where belonging can happen naturally. Because when a child finds what they're built for, the world stops feeling like a place they have to survive.

It starts to feel like a place they can build.

Chapter 18: Build Our Family Operating System

Turn chaos into a repeatable plan – so our home runs on clarity, not crisis

Reader note: This chapter is educational and practical. It does not replace medical or clinical guidance. Use it to collaborate with your BCBA/clinical team and to build a support model that's sustainable for your family.

The Truth Nobody Says Out Loud

Most families don't struggle because they "aren't doing enough." They struggle because the world expects them to run a complex, high-stakes life on improvisation. If you live in a dynamic, high-demand environment—tight schedules, professional obligations, a city that overwhelms the senses—improvisation becomes a silent destroyer. It turns normal stress into chronic crisis. It forces you to make too many decisions under pressure. It drains you until everything feels fragile: your patience, your marriage, your energy, your ability to be kind to yourself. And it leaves my nervous system without a predictable rhythm to borrow.

A bespoke support model means my care is built around realities that don't fit inside a generic therapy template: my nervous system, your lifestyle, and your city context. When support fits real life, progress becomes sustainable. When it doesn't, even "good therapy" collapses.

What you're building in this chapter is a repeatable plan. Not a pretty plan. Not an idealized plan that works only when everyone is well-rested and polite. A plan that still functions on hard days—when someone is dysregulated, when work runs late, when the school calls, when a public moment goes sideways, when the week gets hit by real life.

The Bespoke ABA Blueprint (8 Parts)

This is the operating system. Not a philosophy. A practical build. Eight parts that fit together like a framework you can live inside.

PART 1 — Define "Winning"
(90-Day Outcomes Map)

Start with outcomes across three environments. Then choose only three for the next 90 days. Most families burn out because they try to "fix autism" instead of stabilizing life. Stabilization begins when you define what success looks like in your home, in school, and in the community—then you narrow it down ruthlessly. This is how you stop chasing everything and start building momentum.

Home outcomes (examples)

- Morning routine without crisis
- Bath/bed routine with predictable transitions
- Mealtime stability
- Safe, calm "reset" after school

School outcomes (examples)

- Attendance stability
- Reduced calls home
- Better communication loop with teachers/support staff

Community outcomes (examples)

- Short grocery store success
- Restaurant success (15 minutes, structured)
- Medical appointment success
- Transit success (if relevant)

RULE: If you choose 12 outcomes, you choose none. Choose 3 and protect your focus.

WORKSHEET: 90-Day Outcomes (Choose 3)

1. _____
2. _____
3. _____

Define success in one sentence each:

- Outcome #1 success looks like: _____
- Outcome #2 success looks like: _____
- Outcome #3 success looks like: _____

This part matters because it prevents the family from being swallowed by endless targets. It also gives your BCBA and support team a clear signal: "This is what we're building toward right now."

PART 2 — Find the Real Drivers

(Behavior Economics of Your Home)

Before changing behavior, identify what fuels it. A house without a driver map becomes a house that reacts. And reaction is expensive. Reaction drains marriage. Reaction drains siblings. Reaction drains you. The operating system starts by locating the underlying drivers that keep recurring escalations alive. Most recurring escalations are tied to:

- Transitions
- Sensory overload
- Communication breakdown
- Demand intolerance / task avoidance
- Sleep/hunger cycles
- Unpredictability

WORKSHEET: Trigger Pattern Scan

- What time does it usually happen? _____
- Where does it usually happen? _____
- What's usually true right before it happens? _____
- What does your child get/avoid by doing it? _____
- What helps the fastest (even temporarily)? _____

Operator takeaway: You're not "excusing" behavior—you're building a plan that works. When you do this scan honestly, you stop being surprised by the same episodes. You start seeing patterns. And once you can predict patterns, you can build prevention. Prevention is the foundation of peace.

PART 3 — Design the Weekly Rhythm

(Calendar Architecture)

Urban families collapse when the calendar becomes a battlefield. Most families try to solve chaos with "more therapy." That approach often backfires because it turns the home into a treatment facility. Therapy becomes the only organizing principle. Relationships become secondary. Recovery disappears. And then, ironically, the child becomes more dysregulated because the family system is strained.

Instead, build your week in three layers:

1. Non-negotiables (school/work/sleep windows)
2. Support blocks (ABA sessions, parent coaching, OT/speech)
3. Protection blocks (marriage time, sibling time, parent recovery)

RULE: If you only schedule therapy, your family becomes a treatment facility. You are building a home.

WORKSHEET: Weekly Rhythm (Simple Grid)

- Non-negotiables: _____
- Support blocks: _____
- Protection blocks: _____

Minimum viable week (for travel, stress, chaos):

- Bedtime anchor: _____
- Morning anchor: _____
- Regulation block daily (10–20 min): _____
- Food/hydration baseline: _____

The operating system only works if it survives real weeks—travel weeks, sick weeks, chaotic weeks. That's why the "minimum viable week" is so important. It keeps the floor from dropping out when life gets loud.

PART 4 — Build Your Support Team Like a Small Company

(Roles + Rules)

Your child is the mission. Your family is the enterprise. This is where parents reclaim power. Not controlling power—operational power. Because without clear roles, everyone ends up frustrated. Clinicians blame parents for inconsistency. Parents blame staff for unreliability. The child gets mixed messages. And the house returns to chaos.

Core roles:
- **Clinical Lead (BCBA/Clinician)**: programs, targets, supervision, parent coaching
- **Frontline Support (RBT/BT)**: executes plan, builds trust, records data
- **Parent Operator (you)**: sets priorities, protects rhythm, makes plan livable
- **School Partner**: alignment, generalization, communication loop

CHECKLIST: Team Alignment (print + use)

☐ Everyone knows the top 3 outcomes
☐ Everyone uses the same transition language
☐ Everyone knows calming tools and escalation protocol
☐ Privacy boundaries are explicit
☐ School + home communication has a simple routine

A team that isn't aligned becomes another source of stress. A team that is aligned becomes a pressure relief valve. This is how you stop being alone.

PART 5 — The "Bespoke Match" Standard

(Choosing the Right RBT Fit)

Unspoken truth: outcomes rise or fall on fit as much as credentials. In a family like yours, the provider isn't just doing tasks. They are entering your emotional ecosystem. My nervous system will borrow theirs. Your nervous system will respond to theirs. The wrong fit can make the home feel judged, tense, performative. The right fit can make the home feel safe.

Look for:

- Calm nervous system (your child borrows theirs)
- Respectful tone (no shame, no power games)
- Strong boundaries without ego
- Comfort supporting in public/urban settings
- Discretion + privacy maturity

Red flags

- Power struggles, sarcasm, "I'll show them who's boss" energy
- Talking over your child
- Making your home feel judged
- Over-promising fast results
- Unreliable scheduling/communication

Interview prompts (copy/paste):

- "How do you handle a public escalation without shaming the child?"
- "How do you build rapport in the first two sessions?"
- "What does a great session note look like?"
- "How do you support teens differently than young kids?"
- "What do you do if a parent disagrees with your approach?"

This is not about being picky. It's about protecting the environment. Fit is a safety strategy.

PART 6 — Onboarding

(The First 10 Sessions Decide the Next 10 Months)

Treat onboarding like mission-critical training. If you don't train the system, the system trains you—through chaos.

The 1-Page Child Profile (Give to Every Provider)

- Strengths/interests: _____
- Communication style: _____
- Biggest triggers: _____
- Calming tools that work: _____
- Safety risks (bolting/self-harm/aggression): _____
- Top 3 goals (90 days): _____
- Family values + privacy boundaries: _____
- "What never works" list: _____

First 10 sessions sequence (simple + effective)

1–2: Rapport + regulation (low demands)
3–4: Transitions + visual schedule routines
5–6: Tolerance building (small demands, high reinforcement)
7–8: One community practice (short, structured)
9–10: Parent coaching + weekly rhythm lock-in

RULE: Don't chase data before trust. **Trust is the platform**.

Onboarding is where you avoid the "new provider churn" that breaks families. When onboarding is consistent, progress becomes consistent.

PART 7 — Data Without Burnout

(3 Metrics Only)

Most families quit when tracking becomes homework. So don't make it homework. Track only what creates a signal.

Track just three:

1. Frequency (how often the main behavior occurs)
2. Duration (how long the longest escalation lasted)
3. Recovery time (how long to return to regulated baseline)

WORKSHEET: 30-Second Daily Log

- Main behavior count today: _____
- Longest episode (minutes): _____
- Recovery time (minutes): _____
- One note (1 sentence): _____

Operator win: This gives your BCBA clean signals without turning your home into paperwork.

PART 8 — City Reality Plan - if you live in a major urban area

(Crisis Coverage + Privacy + Travel)

Urban environments amplify risk. Your plan must include the realities.

A) Crisis Coverage (define it before it happens)

WORKSHEET: Crisis Definition + Response

- "Crisis" means (for our home): _____
- First contact: _____
- Second: _____
- Reset protocol: _____
- "Stop session" threshold: _____

B) Privacy Boundaries (non-negotiable)

Your household policy (copy/paste)

- No hallway/lobby discussions about behavior
- No photos/video without written consent
- No social media content—ever
- Default phrase for strangers: "Thanks—we're okay."

C) Travel/Work Demands (high-achiever compatible)

If a parent travels or has irregular hours:

- Coverage schedule: _____
- Two backups: _____
- Minimum viable routine for travel weeks: _____

This is how you keep "city life" from constantly re-triggering chaos. You stop getting ambushed by the environment because you planned for it.

The Family Protection Layer

What actually keeps progress alive

Therapy helps your child. Stability helps your whole family endure long enough for therapy to work.

WORKSHEET: The Protection Schedule

- Sibling 1: day/time _____ activity _____
- Sibling 2: day/time _____ activity _____
- Spouse/partner connection: day/time _____
- Parent recovery block: day/time _____

The 90-Day Implementation Plan

Do this in order:

Weeks 1–2: Foundation

☐ Choose top 3 outcomes
☐ Complete trigger pattern scan
☐ Create 1-page child profile
☐ Define minimum viable routine
☐ Set privacy boundaries + crisis definition

Weeks 3–6: Build

☐ Align or hire team using Bespoke Match Standard
☐ Implement first 10 sessions onboarding sequence
☐ Install visual schedules + transition language
☐ Start daily 30-second data log

Weeks 7–10: Generalize

- [ ] One short structured community practice weekly
- [ ] Simple school communication routine
- [ ] Parent coaching emphasizes real-life rhythm, not theory

Weeks 11–12: Stabilize

- [ ] Review metrics with clinical lead
- [ ] Adjust goals and schedule for sustainability
- [ ] Protect the home from becoming "therapy-only life"

What This Gives Your Child—and What It Gives You

This operating system doesn't just reduce behaviors. It builds predictability, safety, independence, confidence, family stability, and a future that doesn't require heroics to survive.

Final truth: My nervous system needs structure. Your family needs a system. Bespoke care means you stop trying to fit your life into someone else's template.

If you live in a dense city environment, use the "City Protocols" in Appendix A to operationalize elevators, sidewalks, transit, restaurants, and public judgment moments with scripts and safety systems.

Closing: Thank You for Learning My Language.

If you've made it to the end of this book, it means you've done something most people never do. You didn't just look for answers. You stayed long enough to learn the question underneath the question. You didn't come here because autism was convenient or tidy or easy to explain at parties. *You came because you love a child whose inner world doesn't always translate cleanly into the outer world.* You came because you've had days that felt like surviving instead of living. You came because you've tried advice that sounded reasonable and still watched it fail in real life. And you came because some quiet part of you knew that what your child needs is not more judgment, not more shame, not more generic solutions, but understanding that is precise enough to become a plan.

So let me start here, in the simplest language I can offer: **thank you**. Thank you for staying. **Thank you for being willing to learn me rather than trying to edit me into someone else.** Autism is not silence. It is not emptiness. It is not the absence of a person. Autism is a different language, spoken through nervous systems, patterns, sensory experiences, and the strange, powerful ways a brain can process the world when it isn't built for the same default settings as everyone else. And the hardest part for families isn't that this language exists. The hardest part is that the world often misreads it. It labels overwhelm "naughty." It calls fear "defiance." It calls self-protection "attitude." It calls difference "disorder," then wonders why a child feels unsafe.

But you've learned something that changes everything: misbehavior and malfunction are not the only explanations for what you see. You've learned to pause long enough to ask what my nervous system is trying to say. You've learned that behavior is information before it is ever a problem. You've learned that meltdowns are not a personality flaw. You've learned that avoidance is often the most honest communication I have. You've learned that rigidity can be a form of safety. You've learned that what looks "too much" to the world is often my body doing the best it can with an environment that asks too much of it.

And maybe, most importantly, you've learned that autism doesn't exist in a vacuum. It lives inside a family. It lives inside marriages and sibling relationships and careers and calendars and bank accounts and sleep patterns. It lives in the pressure points no one sees from the outside: the school meetings that leave you tense before you even sit down, the public moments where strangers turn your child into a moral lesson, the quiet grief of changed dreams, the worry about the future that can steal oxygen from the present. You've learned that these are not side issues. They are part of the story. They are part of the system. And if you want the child to thrive, the family must survive.

That's why this book wasn't written to make you feel inspired for five minutes and then send you back into chaos. **It was written to give you a new lens and a new set of choices.** Not perfect choices. Not choices that guarantee a smooth life. But choices that turn helplessness into leadership. Choices that shift your home from constant reaction into steady design. Choices that replace improvisation with a repeatable rhythm your child can finally borrow.

You've probably noticed something else as you moved through these chapters: **the biggest breakthroughs rarely came from "trying harder." They came from seeing differently.** From understanding that the goal isn't to force me into normalcy. The goal is to build an environment where my strengths can emerge and my struggles don't have to be punished. The goal is not to demand independence like it's a moral achievement. The goal is to grow agency and dignity in whatever form that takes—supported, shared, staged—because a good life has more than one shape.

This is where I want to gently challenge the way many systems teach you to think about help. Traditional clinic models often treat autism care like a service you drop into once or twice a week, like a repair shop where you hand over a problem and hope it comes back fixed. It's not always malicious, and it's not always incompetent. But for many families, it's not enough. It's too generic, too separated from real life, too disconnected from the environment where patterns actually happen. You don't live in a clinic. I don't melt down in a clinic the way I melt down in a grocery store, in a hallway, in a noisy classroom, in a rushed morning, in a crowded elevator, in a long line when my nervous system is already full. Real progress—lasting progress—usually requires support that meets us where life happens, not only where it's easiest to track.

That's why I want you to begin thinking about getting support the way parents of elite athletes think about development. Not because autism is a sport, and not because I need to be turned into a performance project. But because elite families understand something that matters: **potential is protected by precision**. The most promising athletes don't get built by generic training in crowded systems with little personalization. They get built by teams. By coaching that's tailored. By environments designed around strengths and recovery. By plans that adjust based on what the athlete actually experiences, not what a template says they should experience. Your child deserves that level of intentionality.

Autism is a superpower when it is supported properly. And like any superpower, it needs structure. Without structure, intensity turns into overwhelm. Sensitivity turns into pain. Focus turns into rigidity. Originality turns into isolation. But with the right environment—one that honors regulation, communication, safety, and belonging—those same traits can become extraordinary. You've already seen glimpses of it, even if it's been buried under hard days. You've seen the depth. You've seen the honesty. You've seen the surprising intelligence that shows up when the world finally becomes quiet enough for it to surface. You've seen the loyalty and the intensity of love that can exist in an autistic child. You've seen the brilliance that appears when a child feels safe enough to be themselves. That is what this book has been trying to protect. And now we come to the part that matters: **what you do next**.

I don't want you to read this closing chapter and feel a warm ache and then keep doing the same exhausted loop. I want you to act while the insights are still alive in your body. I want you to choose one thing that shifts your home from reactive to intentional. I want you to build a small rhythm that becomes a foundation. I want you to stop waiting for the "perfect time" when life calms down, because life may not calm down on schedule. The calm is something you build, one decision at a time, with the right support around you. If you've learned my language, then you already know what matters most: not perfection, but repeatability. Not intensity, but sustainability. Not appearance, but safety. Not winning public approval, but protecting dignity. Not carrying everything alone, but creating a system where your family can breathe.

You do not have to become superhuman to raise me well. You have to become intentional. You have to stop running the family on improvisation and start running it on clarity. You have to protect the marriage so it can protect the home. You have to protect the siblings so love doesn't become resentment. You have to protect your own rest because your regulation is part of my safety plan. You have to plan for the future not because you are giving up, but because you refuse to let fear steal the present. You have to build a support model that fits the reality you actually live in—your schedule, your city, your values, my nervous system—so progress stops collapsing the moment life gets hard. And through all of it, I want you to remember this: **I don't need you to erase yourself for me.** I need you to be resourced. I need you to be steady. I need you connected enough to be my anchor when my world feels like too much. Your guilt does not protect me. Your collapse would not help me. Your rest is not a betrayal. It is a safety strategy. Your support team is not a luxury. It is the scaffolding that allows my development to unfold without destroying the family it's unfolding inside.

So thank you—for learning my language. Thank you for staying curious. Thank you for refusing to reduce me to a label. Thank you for seeing that autism is not a life sentence when the environment is built with wisdom. Thank you for believing that a different brain can still be a powerful brain. **Thank you for realizing that the real goal is not to make me look normal, but to help me live well—safely, meaningfully, and with belonging.** If you take that understanding and turn it into action—if you build the operating system, protect the family, seek the level of tailored support that matches my potential—then this story doesn't end with survival. It becomes something else.

It becomes a home where I am not constantly in trouble for being overwhelmed. It becomes a family where love is protected by structure. It becomes a future where autism isn't treated like a handicap to hide, but a superpower to develop. And when you build that kind of life with me, I will feel it in every way a child can feel love—through safety, through steadiness, through belonging, and through the quiet, powerful truth that I was never too much. I was simply speaking a different language, waiting for someone brave enough to learn it.

...

Appendix A: The City Protocols (Urban Parenting Operating Playbook)

A. The "Go-Bag" Standard (always ready)

Carry (or keep in stroller/backpack):

- Noise reduction (ear defenders + backup earbuds)
- Chew/fidget options (2–3 types; rotate)
- "Transition object" (small predictable item: keychain, mini figure, fabric square)
- Visual supports: 5-card mini set (STOP / WAIT / BREAK / HOME / TOILET)
- Snack + hydration kit (one "safe" snack + electrolyte packets if tolerated)
- Wipes + change of clothes + zip bag
- ID card (child's name, parent contact, calming strategies, allergy/medical notes)
- Small blanket or hoodie (deep pressure / comfort)

Parent rule: the go-bag is not "extra." It's **urban safety equipment**.

B. The "3-Minute Reset" (for elevators, lobbies, sidewalks)

Use this when you feel escalation.

1. **Body first:** slow exhale + shoulders down (10 seconds)
2. **Reduce inputs:** step to wall/edge, turn body sideways to crowd, lower voice
3. **One instruction:** "Hands on stroller" / "Hold my sleeve" / "Stand on the dot"
4. **Offer the regulated choice:** "Ear muffs or hoodie?" / "Walk or ride?"

C. Elevator Protocol (high trigger zone)

Before entering:

- Script: "Elevator = quiet body. Eyes on the number. Hands on me."
- Give job: "You press the button."

Inside elevator:

- Body placement: child faces wall/door number; you stand between child and others.
- If crowded: "We'll take the next one." (Normalize it. Don't force it.)

If meltdown starts:

- Don't negotiate. Use: "Out. Reset. Try again."
  You're training the building, not just the child.

D. Sidewalk & Crosswalk Protocol

Non-negotiables in cities: boundaries prevent tragedy.

- Rule: "Stop at every corner."
- Visual: "Corner = statue."
- Teach "hand anchor": child holds **your sleeve/backpack strap** (less conflict than hand-holding).
- **If bolting risk:** use a harness/backpack without shame. This is about safety, not optics.

E. Subway / Transit Protocol (if you use it)

Golden rule: transit is exposure **only when you can leave quickly**.

- Start with **1 stop** practice, off-peak.
- Stand near doors but not directly in front.
- Give job: "You hold the route card."
- Escape plan: "If it's too loud, we get off and reset."

If dysregulated: exit at next stop. Your goal is a **successful exit**, not endurance.

F. Restaurant Protocol (the 5-Minute Win)

Urban dining fails when it's treated like "normal." Make it structured.

- Ask for: booth, corner, away from kitchen/bathroom
- Bring: safe snack + fidget + headphones
- Timebox: **15 minutes** max at first
- Give one job: "You place napkins."
- Order fast: familiar + predictable
- Exit script: "You did it. We leave while it's still a win."

G. Neighbor / Public Judgment Protocol (scripts that protect dignity)

Use calm, low volume. Don't explain your child like a case study.

- **Script 1 (short):** "Thanks — we're okay."

- **Script 2 (firm):** "Please give us space."

- **Script 3 (protective):** "My child is disabled. Step back."

- **Script 4 (authority):** "If you continue, I'll call security."

Parent mindset: privacy is a boundary, not a debate.

H. "Urban School & Services" Survival (waitlists + logistics)

- Keep a single **Services Binder** (digital folder + printed one-pager):
    - diagnosis docs, IEP/504, evals, insurance, provider letters, progress notes
- Maintain a **Waitlist Tracker**:
    - org, contact, date called, next follow-up date, status, requirements
- Follow-up cadence: weekly for 4 weeks → then biweekly.
- Use "paper trail language": "Can you confirm receipt and next steps in writing?"

I. The Apartment Sensory Zone Map (small space version)

Create 3 micro-zones:

1. **Regulation zone:** bean bag/blanket, low light, quiet tools
2. **Learning zone:** table, limited items, visual schedule
3. **Movement zone:** mini trampoline/mat/resistance bands

Rule: each zone has **one purpose**. Mixed-purpose spaces fuel chaos.

Appendix B: Is My Child on the Spectrum?

A Parent Observation Checklist for Ages 4–14 (Not a Diagnosis)

Important disclaimer (please read)

This appendix is an **educational observation tool** designed to help you organize patterns you're noticing in your child (ages **4–14**). It **does not diagnose autism**, does not replace professional screening or evaluation, and should not be used to label a child on its own. Many traits on this list can also appear with anxiety, ADHD, learning differences, language delays, trauma/stress, sleep disruption, sensory processing differences, giftedness, hearing/vision issues, or simply normal developmental variation. If your notes raise concern, the safest next step is to talk with your pediatrician (or primary care clinician) and request **standardized screening and appropriate referrals**.

How to use this tool (the safe way)

1. **Observe for 3–6 weeks** across more than one setting (home, school, sports, family events, errands).

2. Check items that are **frequent**, **intense**, or **interfere with daily life** (learning, friendships, self-care, family routines, safety).

3. Write a **1–2 sentence example** next to each item you check.

4. Use the "Next Steps" section to pursue a **safe evaluation pathway**, even if you're not sure what you're seeing yet.

Parent Observation Checklist (Ages 4–14)

Section 1 — Social connection and "social sense"

☐ Struggles to join play/groups without adult help

☐ Misses social cues (tone, facial expressions, sarcasm, personal space)

☐ Talks *at* people more than *with* them (limited back-and-forth)

☐ Seems much younger socially than peers, or "out of sync" in group settings

☐ Difficulty keeping friends (frequent fallouts, misunderstandings)

☐ Prefers adults or much younger kids because peers feel confusing

☐ Becomes overwhelmed in unstructured social settings (recess, lunch, parties)

Notes/examples: _____

Section 2 — Communication (spoken, nonverbal, and pragmatic language)

☐ Very literal interpretation (misses implied meaning, jokes, idioms)

☐ Difficulty with conversation flow (taking turns, staying on topic, reading interest)

☐ Uses unusually formal language for age, or "scripts" from shows/games

☐ Struggles to explain emotions or needs until they escalate

☐ Eye contact is inconsistent or uncomfortable (or used in a "forced" way)

☐ Repeats questions for reassurance rather than information

Notes/examples: _____

Section 3 — Flexibility, change, and transition tolerance

☐ Big distress when plans change (even small changes)

☐ Needs routines to feel okay; "surprises" often lead to shutdown/meltdown

☐ Strong preference for sameness (foods, clothing, routes, order of tasks)

☐ Difficulty transitioning between tasks without prompting or warnings

☐ Gets "stuck" on fairness/rules and cannot move on

Notes/examples: _____

Section 4 — Repetitive behaviors, intense interests, and "stuck loops"

☐ Repetitive movements when excited/stressed (pacing, rocking, hand motions)

☐ Deep, narrow interests that dominate conversation/time (beyond typical hobby focus)

☐ Needs to talk about the same topic repeatedly

☐ Lines up/sorts/organizes objects beyond what's typical for age

☐ Replays the same scenes/games/songs to regulate

☐ Difficulty stopping preferred activities (extreme reactions to "time's up")

Notes/examples: _____

Section 5 — Sensory differences (often hidden in older kids)

☐ Strong reactions to noise, lighting, crowds, smells, or touch

☐ Clothing sensitivity (tags, seams, fabrics) that causes real distress

☐ Food texture/temperature rigidity (not just picky—meltdown-level)

☐ Seeks sensory input (chewing, pressure, spinning, constant movement)

☐ Avoids grooming routines (haircuts, nail trimming, toothbrushing) due to sensory discomfort

Notes/examples: _____

Section 6 — Emotional regulation, anxiety, and recovery time

☐ Meltdowns or shutdowns that are intense or take a long time to recover from

☐ Anxiety around school, transitions, social situations, or performance

☐ Perfectionism that blocks starting or finishing tasks

☐ "After-school restraint collapse" (holds it together all day, explodes at home)

☐ Self-injury or aggression during overwhelm (even if rare)

☐ Frequent stomachaches/headaches that cluster around stressors (school/social)

Notes/examples: _____

Section 7 — Executive function and daily living skills

☐ Difficulty organizing schoolwork, backpack, time, or multi-step tasks

☐ Needs repeated prompting for routines (despite knowing the steps)

☐ Loses items frequently; forgets instructions easily

☐ Struggles with handwriting, planning, or switching attention

☐ Uneven profile: very advanced in some areas, far behind in others

☐ Daily living skills lag (hygiene, getting ready, chores) compared to peers

Notes/examples: _____

Age-anchored red flags (Ages 4–14)

These are **not a diagnosis**. They're "pattern prompts" that often show up when a child is struggling with the same underlying areas: social communication, flexibility, sensory processing, and regulation.

Ages 4–6 (preschool to early elementary)

☐ Repeated difficulty with **interactive play** (pretend play is rigid, parallel play persists, conflicts spike)

☐ Frequent overwhelm during **transitions** (leaving the park, starting bedtime, switching activities)

☐ **Language may exist**, but conversation is one-sided or very literal

☐ Big reactions to **sensory environments** (birthday parties, assemblies, loud bathrooms)

☐ Strong need for sameness in routines, clothing, food, or how things "must be done"

What it can look like day-to-day: a child who is bright and sweet one-on-one, but becomes dysregulated in groups, noisy settings, or when the schedule changes.

Ages 7–10 (elementary years)

- [ ] Social struggles become clearer: frequent **misunderstandings**, bossiness, "rule policing," or being left out

- [ ] "Flexible thinking" is hard: gets stuck on fairness, exactness, or a single right way

- [ ] **Schoolwork friction** increases due to executive function load (multi-step instructions, writing output, transitions)

- [ ] Sensory overwhelm may show as **irritability, avoidance, headaches, exhaustion**, or refusal—not always obvious distress

- [ ] Intense interests become more consuming and can crowd out peer connection

What it can look like day-to-day: a child who can talk endlessly about one topic, excels in facts, but struggles with teamwork, changing rules, or "reading the room."

Ages 11–14 (middle school and early adolescence)

- [ ] Social demands spike (nuance, sarcasm, shifting alliances), and the child may withdraw, mask heavily, or appear "fine" at school but unravel at home

- [ ] Anxiety, depression symptoms, or school refusal can appear if the child feels chronically unsafe socially or sensory-wise

- [ ] **Identity pressure** rises: the child may feel "different" without understanding why

- [ ] Rigidity may attach to grooming, clothing, schedules, online routines, gaming, or specific "safe" activities

- [ ] Executive function challenges become costly: long-term projects, multiple teachers, lockers, changing classrooms

- [ ] Emotional regulation may look like shutdowns (silent, numb, avoidant) rather than visible meltdowns

What it can look like day-to-day: a capable child who is exhausted by school, overwhelmed by social complexity, and increasingly dependent on rigid routines or safe interests to cope.

Interpreting your checklist (a safe, practical rule of thumb)

Consider moving to professional screening/evaluation if:

- [ ] You checked **multiple items across several sections**, and

- [ ] The pattern is **persistent** and appears across settings/time, and/or

- [ ] There is **real impact**: learning, friendships, self-care, family stability, or safety.

Urgent action: If there is **self-harm, threats, elopement/safety risk, or sudden loss of skills**, contact your clinician promptly.

Next steps: the safest path to clarity (without panic)

1. **Make a pediatrician/primary care appointment** and bring this appendix with your examples.

2. Ask for:
    - standardized developmental/behavioral screening, and
    - referral as appropriate (developmental pediatrics, child psychology/neuropsychology, speech-language pathology, occupational therapy).

3. If school is affected, request a school meeting and ask about learning evaluation/support, and social/emotional support (even while you pursue medical evaluation).

4. Start support based on needs (communication, regulation, sensory, executive function) rather than waiting for a label.

A simple script you can use with a clinician

"I'm not trying to diagnose my child from a checklist. I'm seeing persistent patterns in social communication, rigidity/flexibility, sensory responses, and emotional regulation that are impacting daily life. Here are specific examples across settings. I'd like standardized screening and the safest referral pathway for a full evaluation."

Optional: "One-page summary" you can fill out

- Top 3 situations that trigger distress: _____

- Top 3 strengths / interests: _____

- Biggest daily-life impacts (school/home/friends): _____

- What helps recovery: _____

- What makes it worse: _____

Appendix C: De-escalation Scripts (What to Say / Not Say)

De-Escalation Scripts

What to say / What not to say when your child is overwhelmed

This appendix is not about perfect language. It is about protecting safety, dignity, and regulation in moments when logic is unavailable and emotions are loud. When a child is escalated, language does not teach—it either calms or fuels the nervous system. The goal of these scripts is not compliance. The goal is down-regulation first, learning later.

Think of these as *training wheels*. You won't use them verbatim forever. But in high-stress moments, having reliable words prevents accidental harm and gives your child something predictable to anchor to.

How to Use These Scripts

When escalation begins, your child's nervous system is no longer processing meaning the way you are. Tone, pacing, and predictability matter more than content.

Before you speak, remember three rules:

- Fewer words work better than better words
- Neutral tone beats emotional correctness
- Safety and connection come before explanations

If your body is regulated, your words have power. If your body is dysregulated, even perfect words can fail.

1. Early Escalation

Your child is showing signs of overload but is still reachable.

Your goal: reduce demand, signal safety, prevent a full spiral.

What to say:

- "I see this is getting hard."
- "You're not in trouble."
- "We're going to slow this down."
- "You don't have to decide anything right now."
- "Let's take a pause together."
- "I'm here."

These statements work because they remove threat. They don't ask for behavior. They don't demand eye contact, explanation, or compliance. They tell the nervous system it can stand down.

What not to say

- "Calm down."
- "You're fine."
- "This isn't a big deal."
- "Use your words."
- "You know better than this."

Even when said kindly, these phrases increase pressure. They tell the child their internal experience is wrong or inconvenient—exactly what escalated them in the first place.

2. Mid-Escalation

Your child is upset, loud, rigid, or verbally aggressive.

Your goal: contain the moment, prevent harm, maintain connection without feeding intensity.

What to say

- "I won't let anyone get hurt."
- "I can help you with this."
- "We can stop for now."
- "You're safe."
- "I'm staying."

At this stage, clarity beats comfort. These scripts set boundaries without shame. They say: *this moment has limits, but you are not rejected.*

What not to say:

- "If you don't stop, then…"
- "Why are you doing this?"
- "You're embarrassing yourself."
- "This is ridiculous."
- "I'm done with you."

Questions and consequences escalate here. So does language that threatens abandonment—explicitly or emotionally.

3. Peak Escalation

Your child is no longer processing language normally.

Your goal: keep everyone safe and reduce stimulation.
This is not a teaching moment.

What to say (if anything):

- "I've got you."
- "Safe body."
- "I'm here."
- "Breathe."

Use a calm, even voice. Repeat one phrase if needed. Silence is often better than speech.

What not to say:

- Anything complex
- Anything corrective
- Anything sarcastic
- Anything emotional

At peak escalation, language can act like gasoline. If words aren't helping, stop talking.

---

4. After the Storm

Your child has calmed but may feel ashamed, exhausted, or withdrawn.

Your goal: repair, not review.

What to say:

- "That was really hard."
- "You're safe now."
- "We got through it."
- "I still love you."
- "We can talk later."

These statements rebuild trust. They separate the child from the behavior and reduce post-meltdown shame, which is a major driver of future escalation.

What not to say:

- "Do you see what you did?"
- "Next time you better…"
- "That can't happen again."
- "You scared everyone."

Processing comes later—sometimes much later. **Repair always comes first.**

---

5. When You Need to Set a Boundary

Boundaries are essential—but how they're delivered matters.

What to say:

- "I won't let that happen."
- "That's not safe."
- "We're stopping now."
- "I can help, but I won't argue."

These phrases are firm without being punitive. They communicate authority without threat.

What not to say:

- "Because I said so."
- "You're being bad."
- "You're out of control."
- "This is why we can't have nice things."

Shame-based boundaries may stop behavior short-term, but they increase fear and resentment long-term.

---

6. Scripts for Public Settings

When eyes are on you and pressure is high.

To your child:

- "We're leaving."
- "You're not in trouble."
- "I've got this."
- "We'll try again another time."

To bystanders:

- "Thanks—we're okay."
- "We've got it handled."

Short, closed scripts protect privacy and reduce your own stress. You do not owe anyone an explanation.

7. Scripts for Yourself

Because your regulation matters too.

- "This is hard, not hopeless."
- "I don't need to fix everything right now."
- "I can handle this moment."
- "I can repair myself later."

Parents escalate too—internally or externally. Having words for yourself keeps the situation from spiraling further.

Final Note

These scripts are not magic. They won't prevent every meltdown. But they do something powerful: they remove accidental harm. They keep your words from becoming another threat your child has to survive.

When you consistently speak in ways that reduce pressure instead of adding it, your child learns something profound: *Even when I lose control, I am still safe in this relationship.*

That belief—more than any technique—is what ultimately reduces escalation over time.

Appendix D: Sensory Audit Checklist

A practical tool to reduce overload before it becomes behavior

This checklist helps you identify sensory stressors that quietly tax your child's nervous system—and your family's—long before a meltdown occurs. It is not about eliminating stimulation. It's about reducing unnecessary load so your child has more capacity for learning, flexibility, and connection.

Use this audit quarterly, during growth spurts, or whenever behavior changes without an obvious cause.

How to Use This Checklist

- Walk through each section during a calm moment, not during a crisis.
- Check what applies most days, not only on worst days.
- Prioritize fixes that are low effort, high relief.
- Remember: one small change can lower the entire system's stress.

PART 1: Home Sensory Audit

A. Sound

☐ TVs, radios, or devices run in the background most of the day
☐ Multiple people talk at once during routines
☐ Sudden loud sounds (appliances, door slams, alarms) are common

- ☐ Echoes or hard surfaces amplify noise
- ☐ Child covers ears, hums, yells, or flees during noise

Quick wins:

- Designate quiet hours
- Use soft-close hardware
- Add rugs, curtains, or white noise
- Give advance warning before loud sounds

B. Light & Visual Load

- ☐ Overhead lighting is bright or flickering
- ☐ Screens are always on or visible
- ☐ Visual clutter (toys, papers, decor) fills shared spaces
- ☐ Rapid visual transitions (TV edits, scrolling) occur often
- ☐ Child squints, avoids rooms, or becomes hyperactive under lights

Quick wins:

- Switch to warm, indirect lighting
- Reduce visual clutter in high-use areas
- Create a low-stimulation "reset space"

C. Touch & Clothing

☐ Tags, seams, or fabrics cause irritation
☐ Clothing changes trigger distress
☐ Haircuts, nail trimming, or bathing escalate quickly
☐ Child avoids certain furniture or textures
☐ Physical closeness becomes aversive during stress

Quick wins:

- Standardize favorite clothing textures

- Pre-warm towels; use pressure before touch

- Offer choice and predictability around care tasks

D. Smell & Taste

☐ Strong cooking, cleaning, or fragrance smells linger
☐ Child avoids rooms during food prep
☐ Mealtime escalates without obvious cause
☐ Child gags or refuses foods unpredictably

Quick wins:

- Ventilate during cooking

- Use unscented products

- Keep "safe foods" reliably available

E. Movement & Body Awareness

☐ Long sitting periods are expected
☐ Transitions happen without movement breaks
☐ Child crashes, spins, paces, or seeks pressure
☐ Dysregulation increases after school or car rides

Quick wins:

- Schedule movement before demands

- Use heavy work (pushing, carrying, squeezing)

- Normalize pacing or rocking as regulation

PART 2: Routine & Transition Load (Home)

☐ Mornings feel rushed or unpredictable
☐ Transitions happen verbally without visual cues
☐ Expectations change day-to-day
☐ Child is surprised by demands
☐ Dysregulation spikes during transitions

Quick wins:

- Use visual schedules

- Give countdowns ("5 minutes, 2 minutes")

- Keep routines consistent even on weekends

PART 3: Outings Sensory Audit

A. Preparation

☐ Outings happen with little warning
☐ Child doesn't know how long they'll be out
☐ No clear exit plan exists
☐ Hunger, thirst, or fatigue aren't addressed beforehand

Quick wins:

- Preview the outing verbally or visually

- Set a time limit ("15 minutes")

- Pack regulation tools and snacks

B. Transportation

☐ Car noise or motion causes distress
☐ Traffic or stops increase agitation
☐ Entry/exit from vehicles is rushed
☐ Child arrives dysregulated before the outing begins

Quick wins:

- Quiet music or silence

- Weighted lap pad or compression

- Build decompression time after arrival

C. Public Spaces

- ☐ Bright lighting (stores, offices) overwhelms
- ☐ Crowds trigger vigilance or panic
- ☐ Unexpected touch occurs
- ☐ Smells, noise, and visual input stack quickly

Quick wins:

- Shop during off-peak hours
- Use noise-reducing headphones
- Stand near exits
- Limit time on first attempts

D. Social & Performance Pressure

- ☐ Child is expected to "behave" for others
- ☐ Public correction happens
- ☐ Attention from strangers increases stress
- ☐ Child masks until they collapse later

Quick wins:

- Remove performance expectations
- Use private cues instead of public correction
- End outings early without shame

PART 4: Cumulative Load Check

☐ Multiple stressors occur before escalation
☐ Meltdowns happen after "successful" days
☐ Recovery time is increasing
☐ Child seems exhausted, not defiant

Operator insight:
Escalation is often the result of stacked sensory debt, not a single trigger.

Final Review: Choose 3 Adjustments

Circle or write the three easiest changes you can make this week:

1. _____
2. _____
3. _____

Small reductions in sensory load create outsized gains in regulation, learning, and safety.

Closing Note

This audit is not about removing challenges from your child's life. It's about removing unnecessary friction so your child's energy can be spent on growth instead of survival.

When the environment becomes calmer, your child doesn't become weaker. They become *more available*—to learn, to connect, and to thrive.

Appendix E: School / IEP Meeting Prep Sheet

A practical guide to walk into meetings calm, clear, and in control

This prep sheet is designed to help you enter school and IEP meetings regulated, prepared, and positioned as a collaborative authority, not a reactive advocate. The goal is not to "win" a meeting. The goal is to secure supports that actually work in real life—while protecting your child's dignity and your family's energy.

Use this sheet the night before or the morning of any school-related meeting.

PART 1: Re-anchor Yourself Before the Meeting

School meetings often trigger defensiveness because parents are used to being misunderstood, rushed, or subtly judged. Before preparing content, prepare your nervous system.

Grounding check (30 seconds):

- My goal is clarity, not conflict.
- I am the expert on my child.
- This meeting is about fit, not fault.

Write one sentence you want to remember if the meeting becomes tense:

PART 2: Define the Purpose of This Meeting

Meetings go off-track when the purpose isn't explicit. Primary reason for today's meeting (circle one):

- Initial IEP / eligibility
- Annual review
- Behavior concerns
- Placement discussion
- Services adjustment
- Crisis response
- Transition planning

One-sentence purpose statement:

"Today, I want us to focus on _____."

If nothing else is accomplished, *this* is what must be addressed.

PART 3: Child Snapshot (Bring the Whole Child Into the Room)

Schools often meet paperwork, not people. This snapshot recenters the conversation.

Strengths (academic, social, creative, emotional):

- _____

What motivates my child:

- _____

What dysregulates my child most at school:

- _____

What helps my child regulate at school:

- _____

One thing I want the team to understand about my child as a person:

- _____

PART 4: Current Pain Points (Be Specific, Not Emotional)

Vague concerns get vague responses. Precision gets action.

Top 3 school challenges right now:

1. _____
2. _____
3. _____

For each challenge, note:

- When it happens: _____
- Where it happens: _____
- What usually triggers it: _____
- What currently happens after: _____

This reframes "behavior problems" as environmental mismatches.

PART 5: What You Are Asking For (Clear Requests)

Schools respond best to concrete asks tied to function. Primary supports requested:

☐ Academic accommodation

☐ Behavioral support

☐ Sensory supports

☐ Schedule modification

☐ Staff training

☐ Communication changes

☐ Placement change

☐ Safety plan

Write your top 3 requests clearly:

1. "We are requesting _____."

2. "We are requesting _____."

3. "We are requesting _____."

If possible, link each request to regulation, access, or safety, not performance.

PART 6: Boundaries & Non-Negotiables

It is okay to name limits.

Non-negotiables for our family:

☐ No public shaming or correction

☐ No punitive behavior plans

☐ No removal of supports without data

☐ Clear communication before discipline

☐ Safety-first approach during escalation

Boundary phrase to use if needed:

> "That approach doesn't work for my child. We need an alternative."

PART 7: Anticipate Pushback (So You're Not Caught Off Guard)

Possible school concerns:

- "We don't see that behavior here."
- "We don't have staffing for that."
- "That's not typical."
- "We need to wait and see."

Prepared response:

> "I understand. Here's what we're seeing at home and why this support matters."

You are not required to debate your child's experience.

PART 8: Communication Plan Going Forward

Meetings fail when follow-up is unclear.

Point of contact: _____
Preferred communication method: _____
Frequency of updates: _____

How concerns will be raised before they escalate:

PART 9: End the Meeting With Alignment

Before leaving, summarize.

Ask this question:

> "Can we recap what we agreed to today?"

Write agreed-upon actions:

- School will: _____

- Parents will: _____

- Review date: _____

If something is unclear, ask for it in writing.

PART 10: After-Meeting Reset (For You)

Meetings can be draining even when they go well.

After-meeting care (choose one):

- Walk
- Music
- Quiet
- Call a trusted person
- Do nothing on purpose

You are allowed to decompress.

Closing Note

You do not need to become aggressive to be effective. Calm clarity is powerful. When you walk into school meetings prepared, grounded, and specific, the dynamic shifts. You move from being "the worried parent" to being a strategic partner.

This sheet exists to help you protect your child *and* yourself—so advocacy does not become another source of burnout.

Continue Your Journey

You Don't Have to Do This Alone

If this book resonated with you, it's because you're living this reality—not reading it from the outside.

Who Is BSP Solutions?

BSP stands for **Best Supported** and **Prepared** (for life).
BSP Solutions exists to help families affected by autism move from:

- constant crisis
- emotional isolation
- decision fatigue
- burnout

➡ into structure, clarity, and confidence.

We don't offer judgment.
We don't offer generic advice.
We help families build real-world systems that work.

Your Next Step (It's Free)

Scan the QR code below, and you'll be guided to our private entry page.

There, you can:

✔ Get free access to practical tools you can use immediately
✔ Join our live and on-demand webinars for parents
✔ Schedule a consultation to learn more about BSP Solutions Membership offers
✔ Decide your pace—no pressure, no obligation

Start Here

Scan the QR Code Below

What Happens After You Scan?

No spam.
No selling your data.
No overwhelm. Just an invitation to elevated levels of support.

A Final Word From the Author

You were never meant to figure this out by yourself.

Strong families don't survive because they try harder.
They survive because they build support systems that evolve with them.

Whether you take one small step today or simply bookmark this for later—you are welcome here.

With respect and solidarity,

- Ray E.
Founder & CEO, BSP Solutions
Best Supported and Prepared (for life)

• • •